Pat Collins CM

Mind and Spirit

PSYCHOLOGY AND SPIRITUALITY IN DIALOGUE

D1264548

the columba press

First published in 2006 by
the columba press
55A Spruce Avenue, Stillorgan Industrial Park,
Blackrock, Co Dublin

Cover by Bill Bolger
Origination by The Columba Press
Printed in Ireland by ColourBooks Ltd, Dublin

ISBN 1 85607 542 7

Table of Contents

Preface

I would like to put the preface of this important book in a personal context. In 1945 at the age of 16, I was attending a retreat in Birmingham run by the Jesuits. The retreat master asked me what I was going to do after leaving school and I replied I hoped to train to be a doctor. 'What kind of doctor?' he asked and I replied, 'A psychiatrist.' The colour of his face changed, becoming ashen white. He waved his finger at me and solemnly declared that this was the quickest way to lose my faith and my soul. I thanked him for his advice and duly proceeded to become a psychiatrist. I am now certain that if I had not become a psychiatrist, I would have lost my faith. It is still too early to know what will happen to my soul.

What is certain is that in the last sixty years the practice of the faith that priest was familiar with has nearly collapsed. Today we are facing a church that is haemorrhaging in attendance numbers and its members are seriously disenchanted with its emphasis on a theology of dogmas, creeds and the black and white certainty of the rules of its official teaching.

Instead there has been a meteoric rise in interest in spirituality shown in survey after survey. Spirituality lies at the very opposite end of the spectrum of the previous era of spiritual clarity of rules and regulation, certainty, and a religious experience dominated by the external. Instead it is saturated by the internal world of feelings, emotions, the mystical, the subjective, the ecstatic, and the spirit and most important of all, love! This is not the world of the certainty of reason of Thomas Aquinas, although it embraces it too. It is a very difficult world of an interaction between psychology and spirituality. It needs careful unpacking and that is precisely what this book does.

In eleven brief chapters it summarises the essential contributions of psychology and spirituality. Transpersonal psychology, health, happiness and spirituality, the spiritual basis of

Alcoholics Anonymous, the paranormal, the contribution of neuroscience, near death experiences and many others are all covered simply and in condensed form.

This is not a textbook of the subject, but a very useful and erudite introduction for the vast array of interested participants.

Jack Dominian

Introduction

There is a story that I like very much. It is about a clergyman who was suffering from a nervous breakdown. He went to Dr Carl Jung seeking help. The famous Swiss psychologist quickly noticed that the unfortunate man was suffering from elevated levels of stress due to a fourteen hour working day. Jung's advice was quite simple. The minister was to work eight hours a day and then go home to spend the evening quietly on his own. Since the man was in real distress, he made up his mind to follow the instructions to the letter. Having worked eight hours he returned home, had his supper, and then went into his study and closed the door. He played a few records and finished reading a novel. The next day was much the same, except that during his time alone he began another novel and listened to some more music. On the following morning he went back to Dr Jung who asked him how he was feeling.

When he complained that he was no better, Jung asked him what exactly he had done. When he heard a detailed account Jung retorted, 'But you didn't understand. I didn't want you with novelists or composers. I wanted you to be all alone with yourself.' At this the poor clergyman looked scared, and said: 'Oh, but I can't think of worse company!' To which Jung gave this classic reply, 'And yet this is the self you inflict on other people fourteen hours a day.'

In a way this vignette encapsulates the way in which psychology and spirituality can complement one another. Jung analysed the clergyman's problem in a psychological way as a lack of self-acceptance and low self-esteem, but proposed a spiritual answer when he encouraged him to have a daily quiet time.

The Sounds of Silence
Silence is a key notion in spirituality. St John of the Cross explained the reason why: 'The Father uttered one Word; that

Word is his Son, and he utters him forever in everlasting silence; and in silence the soul has to hear it.' One of the reasons why the presence of God is eclipsed in modern culture is the fact that there is noise rather than silence. Speaking about it, T. S. Eliot wrote in *Choruses From the Rock:* 'The endless cycle of idea and action, endless invention, endless experiment, brings knowledge of motion, but not of stillness; knowledge of speech, but not of silence; knowledge of words, and ignorance of the Word.'[1] In *The Perennial Philosophy*, Aldous Huxley said that there are three kinds of silence, silence of the mouth, silence of the mind, and silence of the will. But Huxley observed: 'Our era is among other things, the Age of Noise. Physical noise, mental noise and the noise of desire.'[2] Let's look briefly at each of them.

Firstly, there is the phenomenon of physical noise. All the modern media such as radio, TV, MP3 players, mobile phones, e-mails, text messages and the internet tend to banish silence. The din goes far deeper than the ear drums, observed Huxley. 'It penetrates the mind, filling it with a babel of distractions – news items, mutually irrelevant bits of information, blasts of sentimental music, and continually repeated doses of drama that bring no catharsis.'[3]

Secondly, there is the problem of mental noise. When I run courses on stress reduction I teach people how to do relaxation exercises. A number of them encourage participants to learn how to pay sustained attention to one thing. It might be a candle flame, a mantra, or on a physical sensation, such as warmth in one's hands or feet. What most people quickly discover is that they find it very hard to concentrate on any one thing for more than a few seconds. Like a restless grasshopper their minds jump from one idea to another.

Thirdly, there is, what could be referred to as silence of the will. This occurs when we no longer are agitated by a succession of worldly desires for things like popularity, pleasure power

---

1. *Selected Poems* (London: Faber & Faber, 1969), 107.
2. (London: Fontana, 1966), 225.
3. *The Perennial Philosophy* op. cit., 225.

and possessions. As the chapter on Alcoholics Anonymous points out, worldly desires nail down our spiritual energies to created things in such a way that they are no longer available for relationship with God. Resulting attachments can develop into addictions. As Gerald May says in his book *Addiction and Grace*, in modern culture the question is not so much, 'have you an addiction?' But rather, 'what addictions have you got?'

Pope Paul VI spoke eloquently about the spiritual consequences of lack of silence. 'Today our psychology is turned outward too much. The exterior scene is so absorbing that our attention is mainly directed outside; we are nearly always absent from our personal abode. We are unable to meditate or pray. We cannot silence the hubbub inside, due to outside interests, images, passions. There is no quiet, holy space in the heart for the coming of God.'[4] During Advent 2002, John Paul II, observed that as a result of the noisy distractions already mentioned, many people were losing touch with God. This theme will be explored in the chapter on atheism. It is not surprising, therefore, that nowadays numerous men and women complain about the silence of God. In his book *Crossing the Threshold of Hope* John Paul wrote: 'It is truly difficult to speak of the silence of God. We must speak, rather, of the desire to stifle the voice of God.'[5]

So if we want to savour the ultimate meaning and mystery of life we need to lessen physical, mental, and volitional noise. We need appointments with ourselves, times of quiet when we try to listen to the deeper things of our own hearts. It is at times like these that the voice of God can be heard in the deeper personality, in the form of longings to experience the presence and purposes of God. There is no religious experience without such preceding desire. The deeper and stronger the desire the greater the subsequent awareness of God will be.

---

4. Edward O' Connor, *Pope Paul and the Spirit* (Notre Dame: Ave Maria Press, 1978), 69.
5. (London: Jonathan Cape, 1994), 130.

Religious Experience and Spirituality

Religious experience lies at the heart of religion and spirituality. The word religion is defined in the first chapter. As for spirituality, it is notoriously difficult to define. Bernard Mc Ginn says that without making an exhaustive search he turned up 35 different definitions.[6] Spirituality can refer to three main areas: personal religious experience; the inspiration that binds a group together e.g. Franciscan or Celtic spirituality; or an academic study of the previous two. That said, there are two main ways of defining spirituality: firstly, a general definition that embraces theistic and non-theistic forms, and secondly, a specifically theistic/ Christian one. Sandra Schneiders provides us with a general definition when she describes spirituality as 'conscious involvement in the project of life integration through self-transcendence toward the ultimate value one perceives.'[7] Speaking about specifically Christian spirituality Michael Downey has written: 'It is a way of living for God in Christ through the presence and power of the Holy Spirit.'[8]

In recent years many people have become disillusioned with institutional religion. There are numerous reasons why this is so, ranging from secularisation, and authoritarianism, to church scandals. Suffice it to say that nowadays lots of people say that, although they are not religious, in terms of the objective religious elements of the Christian religion such as its beliefs and ethics, they are spiritual. Even when they don't define what they mean by the words spiritual and spirituality, they seem to be referring to the importance of non material values and beliefs in their lives. In recent years there has been an enormous growth in alternative spiritualities. People who are seekers, enter the supermarket of meaning and pick and choose the spiritual ideas

6. 'The Letter and the Spirit: Spirituality as an Academic Discipline' *Finding the Spirit: The Study of Christian Spirituality*, Ed. Dreyer & Burrows, (Baltimore & London: The John Hopkins University Press, 2005), 29.
7. 'Christian Spirituality: Definition, Methods and Types', *The New SCM Dictionary of Christian Spirituality* (London: SCM, 2005), 1.
8. *Understanding Christian Spirituality* (New York: Paulist Press, 1997), 43.

and practices that, hopefully, will be relevant and helpful to them. Topics on offer range from dream interpretation, journal writing, caring for the soul, the Enneagram, spiritual direction, yoga, Tai Chi, Reiki healing, shamanism, angelology and many New Age practices. They often read authors whose writings have a psycho-spiritual orientation such as Scott Peck's, *The Road Less Travelled*, Thomas Moore's *Care of the Soul: A Guide to Cultivating Depth and Sacredness in Everyday Life*, Gerald May's *Addiction and Grace*, and Jack Dominian's *One Like Us: A Psychological Interpretation of Jesus*. Many of these contemporary pilgrims are engaged in a spiritual quest, to use Batson's term.[9]

I have long believed that religious experience as conscious awareness of the higher Power is not only spiritual; it is, to use James Pratt's terminology, either mildly or intensely mystical.[10] Speaking of the awareness of mystery Pratt said that it was 'the sense of the presence of a being or reality through other means than the ordinary perceptive processes or reason.'[11]

There is some justification for the contemporary distinction between religion and spirituality when the word religion refers only to its objective elements such as creeds and rituals rather than its subjective, experiential components. However, there is no justification for the widespread impression that spirituality is somehow incompatible with organised religion. There is overwhelming evidence to the contrary. Christianity has a wonderful ascetical tradition, stretching from the scriptures through the wisdom of the Eastern and Western churches to the great saints of more recent centuries. As loyal members of the church the saints were nourished by its teachings, liturgy and traditions which not only enabled them to grow in holiness of life, but also inspired their many writings.

---

9. Cf Batson & Schoenrade, 'Quest Scale', *Measures of Religiosity*, ed. Hill & Hood, (Birmingham, Alabama: Religious Education Press, 1999), 138-141.
10. *The Religious Consciousness: A Psychological Study* (New York: Macmillan, 1920), 337.
11. Cf *The Religious Consciousness: A Psychological Study* op. cit., 37.

Science and Spirituality

In the modern world, religion and spirituality exist in an environment which has become increasingly influenced by science and technology. Their combined achievements over the last few hundred years have been most impressive. Currently, there are a number of excellent books which document those achievements.[12] Psychology, including the psychology of religion, is part of that success. But from the time of Galileo Galilei (1564-1642) there has been a tension between religion and science, and *ipso facto* between religion and psychology. But I have always thought that the conflict is more apparent than real. I agree with what Galileo wrote: 'I think that in the discussion of natural problems, we ought not to begin at the authority of scripture, but at sensible experiments and necessary demonstrations. *For, from the Divine Word, the sacred scripture and nature did both alike proceed.*' He went on to say that if scripture seemed to be in conflict with scientific findings it was probably due to the fact that the scriptures were being misinterpreted. He concluded, 'Nor does God less admirably discover himself to us in nature's actions, than in the scriptures' sacred sayings.'[13] If that is true in a general sense, it necessarily follows that there is no essential conflict between psychology and spirituality.

Despite the undoubted tensions that exist between the two subjects, I'm convinced that psychology has a lot to contribute to a more accurate and insightful grasp of spirituality and *vice versa*. In the past I have written about a number of psycho-spiritual topics.[14] Although this book continues to explore the rela-

---

12. Cf. Isaac Asimov, *Asimov's New Guide to Science* (London: Penguin, 1987); John Gribbin, *Science: A History 1543-2001* (London: Penguin, 2003); Brian Greene, *The Fabric of the Cosmos* (London: Penguin, 2004); Bill Bryson, *A Short History of Nearly Everything* (London: Black Swan, 2003)

13. Bronowski & Maslish, *The Western Intellectual Tradition*, (London: Penguin, 1963), 153.

14. 'Self-esteem and the love of God', *Growing in Health and Grace* (Galway: Campus, 1991), 27-43; 'Reducing Stress and Finding Peace' (Dublin: Veritas, 2002); 'Is Prayer Good for your Health?' *The Broken Image* (Dublin: Columba, 2002), 86-92; 'Dreams: a Christian Under-

tionship of psychology and spirituality it is not a systematic, and comprehensive treatment. The constraints of space, knowledge and ability have ruled out that possibility. What I have chosen to do is to tackle a number of subjects which are problematic and interesting. While I have tried to adopt a catholic approach, one which is open to truth wherever it is to be found, the book reflects my specifically Catholic convictions. I should also point out that I am not a trained psychologist. My knowledge is that of a person who has taken a keen interest in the subject over many years. I particularly want to thank Drs Joseph Mc Cann CM and Raymond Topley of the religious studies department of St Patrick's College in Dublin, for their encouragement over a number of years. I also want to thank my students who not only attended my Psychology of Religion lectures but who also sharpened my thinking as a result of their probing and stimulating questions and sharings. It is my hope that, in spite of the complex and academic nature of some of the material, the book will be of help, not only to third level students, but also to thoughtful people who are interested in the synergy that can exist between modern psychology and spirituality.

---

standing' *Growing in Health and Grace* op. cit., 72-86; 'To the Devil with Psychology' *Unveiling the Heart* (Dublin: Veritas, 1995), 26-30; 'Me and my Shadow', *Intimacy and the Hungers of the Heart* (Dublin: Columba, 1992), 74-86; 'The Golden Rule and Empathy', *The Broken Image* op. cit., 21-40; 'Healthy and Unhealthy forms of Guilt' *The Joy of Belonging* (Galway: Campus, 1993), 31-35.

CHAPTER ONE

Psychology and Religion:
An Uneasy Relationship

In the past, hard-nosed science has often seemed to be the implacable enemy of religion. When St Thérèse of Lisieux was tempted to adopt an unbelieving materialism, she echoed the suspicion of many when she admitted: 'The reasoning of the worst materialists is imposed on my mind. Science which makes unceasing advances will eventually explain everything naturally. We shall have the absolute explanation for everything that exists and that still remains a problem, because very many things remain yet to be discovered.' In recent years, however, things have begun to change. Not only have some writers pointed to the spirituality implicit in science's single-minded quest for understanding, they have also drawn attention to the way science has also supported spirituality's subjective claims by providing objective empirical evidence which tends to verify them. This chapter, like the rest of the book, will focus on the, so called, psychology of religion as a branch of the human sciences. It will examine what benefits and dangers may be implicit in a relationship of religion/spirituality and psychology.

Religion and Religious Experience
Our English word 'religion' comes from the Latin *religiare* meaning 'to bind'. Religions bind their members to one another and to the higher Power, i.e. God. They usually have scriptures which would include the Bibles of Christians and Jews, the Koran of Muslims, and the Vedas of Hindus. They express the experience of the founding member/s of the religion and define the limits of orthodoxy, i.e. what is in accord with the foundational experience and what is not. Religions also have such things as forms of worship and ethical codes. All religions, whether theistic like

Christianity or non-theistic like Buddhism are ways of salvation. They aim to liberate people from the forces of evil and oppression whether spiritual or social. At the heart of any religion are religious experiences. William James famously said, in a way which owes a clear debt to Protestant theologian Friederich Schleiermacher (1768-1834), that religious experiences are made up of: 'the feelings, acts and experiences of individual men in their solitude, so far as they apprehend themselves to stand in relation to whatever they may consider divine.'[1] It is from such experiences he says, that theologies, philosophies and ecclesiastical organisations may grow in a secondary way.

Carl Jung also felt that religious experience was important. In his Terry lectures delivered in Yale in 1937 he said that no matter what the world thinks about religious experience, the one who has it possesses a great treasure, a thing that has become for him or her a source of life, meaning and beauty. It has also given a new splendour to the world and to mankind. Having said that religious experience nurtures trust and peace, he asked where was the criterion by which you could say that such a life was not legitimate, and that such an experience was not valid, and that such a faith was mere illusion? Is there, as a matter of fact, any better truth about the ultimate nature of things than the one that helps a person to live? He went on to say: 'No one can know what the ultimate things are. We must therefore take them as we experience them. And if such experience helps to make life healthier, more beautiful, more complete and more satisfactory to yourself and to those you love, you may safely say: "This was the grace of God".'[2] There are clear indications in this quote that William James influenced Jung. The noted American psychologist was a pragmatist who evaluated religion on the basis of its usefulness rather than its truth claims.

---

1. *The Varieties of Religious Experience* (London: Fontana, 1971), 50.
2. 'Psychology and Religion' in *Collected Works*, vol 11, 2nd ed. (1969), pp 3-105.

Professor Ninian Smart says that there are four interrelated forms of religious experience.[3]

- Firstly, there are the numinous kinds which were described by Rudolf Otto in his *The Idea of the Holy*. They involve a felt sense of the *mysterium tremendum et fascinans* i.e. a mystery that is at once mysterious, awesome and fascinating.[4]
- Secondly, there are mystical experiences, whether theistic or non-theistic, which are usually the outcome of contemplation.
- The third kind of religious experience has been referred to as an experience in which a person feels in a state of unity with nature or with the whole universe. This kind of awareness, which was evident in Wordsworth's poems, is sometimes referred to as nature mysticism.
- Fourthly, there is religious experience in the form of conversion. Sts Paul and Augustine were outstanding examples. William James devoted a good deal of attention to the phenomenon in chapters nine and ten of *The Varieties of Religious Experience*.

Empirical Research on Religious Experience
During the last century a number of researchers examined religious experiences from a scientific point of view. For example, when Sir Alister Hardy, a biologist, retired from his professorship, he set up a Religious Research Unit in Manchester College, Oxford. He wrote articles in newspapers and magazines which provided examples of religious experiences and invited members of the public to send him personal accounts of similar experiences. When Hardy had assessed all the information he received, he wrote a book about his findings entitled, *The Spiritual Nature of Man: A Study of Contemporary Religious Experience*.[5] In

---

3. 'Religious Experience' *Encyclopaedic Handbook of Medical Psychology*, Ed. Stephen Krauss, (London: Butterworths, 1976), 464.
4. (London: Oxford University Press, 1970), 12-24.
5. (New York: Oxford University Press, 1979).

typical scientific fashion, he tried to classify the available material under twelve different headings. Much of the book was devoted to explaining each category, while providing concrete examples drawn from the responses. A number of accounts of religious experiences in the Hardy archive were later published in a book entitled *Seeing the Invisible: Modern Religious and other Transcendent Experiences* which was edited by Meg Maxwell and Verena Tschudin.[6] David Hay also used Hardy's resources when writing his book, *Religious Experience Today: Studying the Facts*. It contains a very interesting section on religious experience in childhood.[7]

The Alister Hardy Religious Research Unit, which is now located in Lampeter University in Wales, has continued its founder's pioneering work and offers post graduate courses on different aspects of religious experience. For instance, in the late 1970s, David Hay, one of Hardy' successors, and Ann Morisy asked a representative sample of British people whether they had ever been aware of, or influenced by a presence or power, whether they called it God or not, which was different from their everyday selves. They found that about 33% of the respondents said that they had such experiences. Some years later in another sample, Hay and Heald found that 48% of the 985 citizens surveyed said they had significant religious experiences.

Around the same time, a number of American researchers did similar work. In 1973, Greeley and Mc Cready of the National Opinion Research Centre, Chicago, asked a sample of American people whether they ever had an ecstatic type experience. 35% said that they had. In 1978, Princeton Religious Research Centre, a subsidiary of Gallup Polls, confirmed the Chicago figures. It asked the following question in interviews: 'How often have you felt as though you were very close to a powerful spiritual force that seemed to lift you out of yourself?' About 35% of the replies said once, or more than once. While it would probably be fair to say that the USA is a more religious country than Britain

---

6. (London: Arkana, 1990).
7. (London: Mobray, 1990), 32-39.

in terms of church going, the percentage of the population claiming to have had religious experience was about the same.

In recent years, Hay and Hunt have repeated the kind of research done in the 1970s. In an article entitled, 'Is Britain's Soul Waking-Up?' published, 24 June 2000, in the *Tablet*, they revealed that over the last quarter of a century, there has been a startling 110% rise in the number of people reporting religious experiences in the UK. They remarked: 'We are in the midst of an explosive spiritual upsurge ... We know, from the research we have done, that most people's spirituality is a long way away from institutional religion. This spirituality has little doctrinal content, and few people have more than the vaguest remnants of religious language to express their experience of God. The phrase we commonly hear is "I definitely believe in Something; there's Something there." Their spirituality is based upon a longing for meaning.'

When one looks at the research done on both sides of the Atlantic, it clearly and indubitably indicates that anything between a third to two thirds of the population claim to have had a significant spiritual experience. That research raises a question. Are people who believe a creed and go to church more likely to have religious experience that those who don't? There is no clear answer. More research is necessary. I would suspect that those whose religion is authoritarian rather than humanitarian, in Erich Fromm's sense,[8] would be less likely to have religious experience. I'd also suspect that those who have intrinsic rather than extrinsic religion in Gordon Allport's sense,[9] would be more likely to have religious experience. What we do know is that people who get a high score on a Personal Orientation Inventory (POI) are more inclined to have peak experiences of a religious kind. This test seems to confirm Maslow's belief that self-actualisation is hindered rather than helped by traditional religious beliefs and practices, especially if they are conservative

---

8. *Psychoanalysis and Religion* (New York: Bantam, 1967), 35-37.
9. Cf David Wulff, *Psychology of Religion: Classic and Contemporary Views* (New York: John Wiley, 1991), 228.

or fundamentalist. Anyone who is interested in empirical research about religion will find it well summarised in an information packed textbook entitled, *The Psychology of Religion: An
Empirical Approach*, which was co-written by Ralph Wood,
Bernard Spilka, Bruce Hunsberger and Richard Gorsuch.[10] Third
level institutions, especially in Ireland, need to conduct similar
research. As someone who is interested in spirituality, it has occurred to me, over the years, that typically, religious experiences
have a fourfold structure.

The Fourfold Structure of Religious Experience
Firstly, religious experience begins in desire. Down the centuries, great spiritual writers have agreed that grace-prompted
desires for ultimate meaning and God are of singular importance
in the spiritual life. As was mentioned in the introduction, there
is no revelation without preceding desire. Scholars have pointed
to gospel texts which make it clear that Jesus focused on such
desires in his ministry. For example, in Jn 1:35-38 John the
Baptist tells two young men that Jesus is the Lamb of God.
'When the two disciples heard him say this, they followed Jesus.
Turning around, Jesus saw them following and asked, "What do
you want?"' Jesus asked this all-important question because he
realised that God reveals the divine purposes in and through
such desires. Thus St Augustine could write: 'The things you desire you cannot see yet. But the desire gives you the capacity, so
that when it does happen that you see, you may be fulfilled ...
This is our life, to be motivated by holy desire.'[11]

   Secondly, desire for God is expressed in self-forgetful attention to the twin bibles of creation and the scriptures. Writing
about this kind of contemplative attitude, Simone Weil stated:
'Attention consists of suspending our thought, leaving it detached, empty and ready to be penetrated by the object. It means
holding in our minds, within reach of this thought, but on a

---

10. (New York: The Guilford Press, 1996)
11. Tr 4, 'A Reading from the Treatise of St Augustine on the First Letter
of St John' Vol 1, *Divine Office* (London: Collins, 1974), 537-539.

lower level and not in contact with it, the diverse knowledge we have acquired and which we are forced to make use of.'[12] God can be revealed when any aspect of the created world is contemplated by a person with transcendental desire. Needless to say, attention to scripture is one of the best way of opening oneself to the presence and purposes of God. As Prov 4:22-23 tells us: 'My child, be attentive to my words; incline your ear to my sayings. Do not let them escape from your sight; keep them within your heart. For they are life to those who find them, and healing to all their flesh.' One of the most effective ways of paying attention to God's self revelation is by engaging in *Lectio Divina*, i.e. sacred reading, a prayer method that can be traced back to St Benedict.

Thirdly, desire filled attention can lead to contemplative moments of revelation. In scripture we have a promise that those who seek God will not be disappointed. As Jer 29:12-14 assures us: 'You will call upon me and come and pray to me, and I will listen to you. You will seek me and find me when you seek me with all your heart. I will be found by you, declares the Lord.' Again in Is 48:6-8 we read: 'From now on I will tell you of new things, of hidden things unknown to you. They are created now, and not long ago; you have not heard of them before today. So you cannot say, "Yes, I knew of them." You have neither heard nor understood; from of old your ear has not been open.' When people pay self-forgetful attention to either the created world or the scriptures there can be epiphany moments when the presence of God is manifested. For instance, as the person ponders the scriptures, God's alive and active word, ceases to be a mere noun on the page and leaps as a lively verb into the heart, with subjective conviction and power. As a result the person has a new awareness of the presence and purposes of the Lord, one that evokes faith within (cf Rom 10:17).

Fourthly, the revelation of God's loving presence and intentions can lead to four interrelated effects. Firstly, the person will experience feelings of consolation such as peace and joy, which are stirred up by the Spirit's activity in and through God's

12. *Waiting on God* (Glasgow: Fontana, 1974), 71-72.

anointed word, whatever form it takes. Secondly, the person can respond in a prayerful way, e.g. by thanking and praising God. Thirdly, the person can respond in a more practical manner, e.g. by being for others what God is for him or her. Fourthly, having initially responded to the revelation of the presence and purposes of God, the person may react in the form of resistance. In other words, s/he backs off, fearing that the implications of the revelation may be too hard to handle. I have found that such resistance is often rooted in the unconscious influence of negative images of God, e.g. the deity is impersonal, demanding, hard to please, and quick to punish.

A Classic Example of Religious Experience

Here is one of the best known descriptions of a religious experience in Western spirituality. It recounts how, in the course of a conversation at Ostia, St Augustine and his mother St Monica shared this mystical awareness.

> Not long before the day on which she was to leave this life – you knew which day it was to be, O Lord, though we did not – my mother and I were alone, leaning from a window which overlooked the garden in the courtyard of the house where we were staying at Ostia. We were waiting there after our long and tiring journey, away from the crowd, to refresh ourselves before our sea-voyage. I believe that what I am going to tell happened through the secret working of your providence. For we were talking alone together and our conversation was serene and joyful. We had forgotten what we had left behind and were intent on what lay before us. In the presence of Truth which is yourself, we were wondering what the eternal life of the saints would be like, that life which no eye has seen, no ear has heard, no human heart conceived. But we laid the lips of our hearts to the heavenly stream that flows from your fountain, the source of all life which is in you, so that as far as it was in our power to do so we might be sprinkled with its waters and in some sense reach an understanding of this great mystery.

Our conversation led us to the conclusion that no bodily pleasure, however great it might be and whatever earthly light might shed luster upon it, was worthy of comparison, or even of mention, beside the happiness of the life of the saints. As the flame of love burned stronger in us and raised us higher toward the eternal God, our thoughts ranged over the whole compass of material things in their various degrees, up to the heavens themselves, from which the sun and the moon and the stars shine down upon the earth. Higher still we climbed, thinking and speaking all the while in wonder at all you have made. At length we came to our own souls and passed beyond them to that place of everlasting plenty, where you feed Israel for ever with the food of truth. There life is that Wisdom by which all these things that we know are made, all things that ever have been and all that are yet to be. But that Wisdom is not made: it is as it has always been and as it will be for ever – or rather, I should not say that it has been or will be, for it simply is, because eternity is not in the past or in the future. And while we spoke of the eternal Wisdom, longing for it and straining for it with all the strength of our hearts, for one fleeting instant we reached out and touched it. Then with a sigh, leaving our spiritual harvest bound to it, we returned to the sound of our own speech, in which each word has a beginning and an ending – far, far different from your Word, our Lord, who abides in himself for ever, yet never grows old and gives new life to all things.[13]

Clearly the four characteristic elements of a genuine religious experience are evident in this account. Firstly, there are indications in Augustine's description of a transcendental desire for unconditional meaning. When the verbs he uses are highlighted it becomes obvious. He says that he and his mother 'had forgotten what we had left behind and were intent on what lay before us.' In other words, they shared an inner yearning for the future joys of heaven. A little later, Augustine says that he and his

13. *Confessions*, Book 9, Chap 10. (London: Penguin Classics, 1973), 196-198.

mother were 'wondering what the life of the saints would be like' ... 'the flame of love burned stronger in us and raised us higher towards the eternal God.' Later again he adds, 'we were longing for Wisdom and straining for it.' These and other references are evidence of strong desire of a spiritual kind. Secondly, both mother and son were self-forgetful 'our thoughts ranged over the whole compass of material things in their various degrees,' he says. They began by quietly contemplating the garden of the house in which they were staying. Then their attention shifted to the prospect of the beatific vision in heaven. Thirdly, desire and attention were satisfied when, as Augustine puts it: 'At last we came to our own souls and passed beyond them to that place of everlasting plenty'. Then speaking of the Wisdom they longed for, Augustine adds in words of almost breathtaking poignancy: 'for one fleeting instant we reached out and touched it.' Evidently, Augustine and Monica, went beyond thoughts and words about heaven to have an ecstatic awareness of heavenly glory. As the autobiography of St Thérèse of Lisieux revealed in the late nineteenth century, she and her sister Celine had a very similar experience as they contemplated the evening sky. She even compared it to the experience of Augustine and Monica.[14] Fourthly, the two African saints responded to the mystical disclosure of God's heavenly glory in different ways. It took away their fear of mortality, in such a way that Monica became detached from worldly things and prepared herself for her death, while Augustine was prepared for their parting.

The Psychology of Religious Experience

The word 'psychology' comes from two Greek words. Firstly there is *psyche* which refers to the soul or mind. Secondly, there is *logos* which refers to meaning. So psychology literally refers to the meaning of the mind. *The Fontana Dictionary of Modern Thought* says that psychology is 'a word variously defined as the study of behavior, or the study of man interacting with his social

---

14. *Autobiography of a Saint* (London: The Harvill Press, 1958), 134-135.

and physical environment.'[15] The aim of the psychology of religion is to express the workings of the mind when it is religious in terms of the mental processes which have been discovered in secular psychology. Psychology, of whatever kind, is a third person, rather than a first person activity. In other words, rather than examining one's own personal experience, e.g. of religion, by and large it looks at other people's experience in an objective and detached way. Han de Wit says in *Contemplative Psychology*: 'Western scientific psychology explicitly states that it is not bound to any religion. It wants to be religiously neutral even when it speaks about religion ... The academic psychology of religion is in fact a psychology about religious phenomena. And a psychology about religion is not necessarily a psychology that belongs to religion. ... Our academic psychology is, in this sense, a psychology belonging to science and emphatically not a psychology of religion.'[16] It would also be true to say that lying on either side of this form of the psychology of religion are two other forms.

Rather than talking about the psychology of religion, it would be more accurate to talk about psychology and religion or the psychology of religious experience, i.e. the subjective ways in which individuals and groups may experience the teachings of particular faiths. W. W. Meissner makes two important observations about the relationship of psychology and religious experiences in the opening chapter of his book *Psychoanalysis and Religious Experience*.[17] Although the grace of God is a supernatural reality, when it influences a human being it may have a discernible effect upon his or her experience. If and when a person is aware of the activity of grace, then that experience can be studied by psychology. 'Whatever else we can say about religious experience, we can postulate that the form of divine intervention does not violate the nature and functioning of man's capacities – grace perfects nature – and that the form of the experi-

---

15. (London: Fontana),508
16. (Pittsburg: Duquesne University Press, 1991), 20; 31.
17. (New Haven: Yale University Press, 1984), 10.

ence is determined significantly by the nature of the psychic organisation and functioning of the person affected.'[18] As a consequence, religious experience is influenced by many factors, especially by early childhood. 'Religious experience,' observes Meissner, 'in common with all areas of human experience, is influenced by and expresses the residues of earlier development.'[19]

In recent years James Fowler has made a useful distinction between faith as a verb and faith as a noun in *Stages of Faith: The Psychology of Human Development and the Quest for Meaning*.[20] It mirrors a distinction already made between objective and subjective religion. Firstly, there is the subjective act of investing faith/trust. It is a universal human act whereby people place trust in objective centres of power, meaning and value beyond themselves which may or may not be religious. For example, if one's life centres entirely around Irish nationalism or communism it would be a secular faith. However, if people invest faith in transcendental reality, often within the context of a particular religion, they have religious faith and experience. The psychology of religion focuses its attention on subjective acts of investing faith rather than the objective doctrines that are believed. As an empirical discipline psychology has very little to say about the truth or falsehood of the teachings of particular faiths whether Jewish, Muslim, Christian etc. As W. W. Meissner has written, 'The psychology of religious experience in fact must pass over the superhuman precisely because it has no resources even to attempt to understand that loftier dimension ... Consequently, we can say that the psychology of religious experience does not pay attention to the formally supernatural or specifically religious qualities of the phenomena it observes, describes and tries to understand ... The psychological approach assumes that in every religious experience there is a specifiable and analysable human dimension.'[21]

---

18. *Psychoanalysis and Religion*, op. cit., 11.
19. *Psychoanalysis and Religion*, op. cit., 14.
20. (San Francisco: Harper & Row, 1981).
21. *Psychoanalysis and Religion*, op. cit., 6; 7.

David Wulff, one of the best known writers on the subject of the psychology of religious experience, says succinctly: 'Strictly conceived, psychology of religion comprises the systematic application of psychological theories and methods to the contents of religious traditions and to the related experiences, attitudes and actions of individuals.'[22] He says that it is mainly concerned with three main areas:

1) Systematic description of religious experience, formation of ideas and images, and practice, both ordinary and exceptional.
2) Theories of the origin and meaning of religious content and expression in individual lives and in the human race as a whole
3) Research on the fruits – the personal and social effects – of the varieties of religious attitudes and experiences.[23]

Wulff also says that: 'Whereas the empirical approach is inherently a psychology of religious persons and is therefore focused on individual differences in piety, the interpretative perspective is foremost a psychology of religious contents and thus seeks the meaning of the images, objects, stories and rituals that together compose the religious traditions.'[24] It is important to appreciate, however, that while psychology can examine the meaning of the contents of religion and their significance for believers, it cannot pronounce on whether they are objectively true or false. For instance an eminent psychologist like Carl Jung looked at the doctrines of the assumption of the Virgin Mary and the transubstantiation of bread and wine into the body and blood of Christ in the eucharist, from this psychological point of view.

Tensions
Over the years I have become aware of three areas where there can be tension between psychology and spirituality as religious experience.

22. 'Psychology of Religion: An Overview', *Religion and Psychology: Mapping the Terrain,* ed Jonte-Pace and Parsons (London: Routledge, 2001), 17.
23. 'Psychology of Religion: An Overview' op. cit. 18.
24. 'Psychology of Religion: An Overview' op. cit. 22.

1. Linguistic and Conceptual confusion

There seems to be considerable confusion in the use of English words such as mind, psyche, and soul. When you look up the authoritative *Oxford English Dictionary*, you find that they have overlapping meanings. I suspect that the linguistic difficulties reflect the fact that in Greco-Roman thought a human being was seen as a combination of body and soul. As Paddy Quinn explains in his *Philosophy of Religion A-Z*, the soul or psyche is seen as that which 'defines human existence as spiritual and intelligent.'[25] What is confusing about this notion is that it doesn't seem to differentiate between the soul as mind, and the animating spirit that is capable of relationship with God.

For the sake of clarity I am going to use words such as body, soul, psyche, mind and spirit in a biblical way in this book, by assigning them specific if slightly arbitrary meanings. In the New Testament there is clear evidence that in Judeo Christian thought, a person is a unity of 1) body, 2) soul/psyche/mind, 3) spirit. For example in 1 Thess 5:23 St Paul prays: 'May the God of peace himself sanctify you entirely; and may your spirit, soul and body be kept sound and blameless at the coming of our Lord Jesus Christ.' It is important to establish clearly what Paul meant by these three words. The body, i.e. *soma* in Greek, refers to our physical make up. It connects us to the universe, other people, and with members of the Body of Christ. The soul, i.e. *psyche* in Greek, is the natural soul, the centre of thought, memory, feeling and willing.[26] The spirit, i.e. *pneuma* in Greek, is the God-given aspect of human nature that is made in the image and likeness of its Maker. Writing about the human spirit, George Montague says: 'If *psyche* is the inward principle of life which animates me, *pneuma* is my self as born from above and facing upward, my openness to self-transcendence, to movement beyond where I now stand.'[27] Because of my respect for biblical

---

25. (Edinburgh: Edinburgh University Press, 2005), 202.
26. In the remainder of this book the word 'soul' will refer to the mind, or *psyche*.
27. 'Body, Soul and Spirit,' *Riding the Wind*, (Ann Arbor, Mich.: Word of Life, 1977), 30.

theology, instead of talking of the traditional trinity of body, mind and soul, I intend to talk about body, mind and spirit in this book.

The linguistic confusion which is evident in the use of words mentioned above, is echoed in the psychology of religion. Because it is an empirical science, psychology concentrates on the material, observable aspects of human nature, namely, body and mind. In literature about the psychology of religious experience, there is a tendency to equate soul and spirit, in such a way that they become virtually synonymous. This confusion is fairly obvious in the writings of Carl Jung. Whereas he believed that human beings were essentially religious and could only be psychologically healthy and fulfilled if they had genuine religious experience, he seemed to locate the sense of spiritual need in the deeper recesses of the collective unconscious. Because he didn't seem to distinguish between the human soul (*psyche*) and the spirit (*pneuma*) he implied that people's religious capacities were located in the instinctual soul as opposed to the spiritual self. Erich Fromm observed: 'Jung reduces religion to a psychological phenomenon and at the same time elevates the unconscious mind to a religious phenomenon.'[28] According to Wouter Hanegraaff, Jung, 'sacralised psychology ... The result was a body of theories which enabled people to talk about God while really meaning their own psyche, and about their own psyche while really meaning the divine. If the psyche is "mind", and God is "mind" as well, then to discuss one must mean to discuss the other.'[29]

2. Psychologising Spirituality

Anyone who reads the Christian classics of bygone centuries will begin to appreciate the fact that some of the great spiritual writers were good psychologists. For instance when one reads what Evagrius Ponticus, Augustine of Hippo, John Cassian and

28. *Psychoanalysis and Religion*, (New York: Bantam, 1967) , 20.
29. Quoted in *Christ the Bearer of the Water of Life: The New Age Evaluated.*

Teresa of Avila, had to say about human passions, one quickly appreciates how keen was their psychological insight. For them however, psychology was the servant of spirituality. But in contemporary culture, there is a danger that spirituality is becoming the servant of psychology. Gerald May – a half brother of Rollo May – is a practising Christian, a psychiatrist, and the author of a number of distinguished books which bring psychology and spirituality together in an enriching way. In his *Will and Spirit: A Contemplative Psychology*, he warns about the danger of psychologising spirituality: 'We have had enough attempts to explain spiritual experience in psychological terms.'[30] May goes on to say that when many people attempt to integrate psychology and spirituality, there is an obvious one-sidedness in the relationship. 'Psychology is felt to be the more "workable" of the two' he observes. 'It offers hard answers and objectifiable techniques. The contributions of religion are either forgotten entirely or considered too esoteric or touchy to be handled. Therefore when the two come together, instead of integration, there is an absorption of religion into psychology. The result is a psychology that may or may not have a few religious trappings.'[31] In the preface of Han de Wit's *Contemplative Psychology*, well known psychologist, Professor Adrian Van Kaam said something similar: 'I have become more and more concerned with the secularisation of Christian spirituality by the eager use of insights and tests developed in human developmental theories and psychologies.'[32]

3. Psychology as Spirituality

The psychologising of religion reaches an extreme degree when it becomes a form of religion/spirituality itself. Historically, this trend can be traced back to *The Essence of Christianity* by Ludwig Feuerbach which was published in 1841. A number of eminent scholars such as Freud, Fromm, Durkheim and Marx adopted Feuerbach's notion of God as a projection of alienated human

---

30. (San Francisco: Harper & Row, 1982), vii.
31. *Will and Spirit*, op. cit., 11.
32. (Pittsburg Pennsylvania, Duquesne University Press, 1991), vii.

potential. It is not surprising, then, that Paul Tillich and Paul Vitz, have echoed a complaint of some twentieth century religious thinkers when they accuse a number of psychologists of replacing religion with a secular form of salvific psychology.[33] Vitz cites Erich Fromm, Carl Rogers, Abraham Maslow and Rollo May as men who tried to replace traditional notions of belief, with a self-glorifying humanism. For example, Abraham Maslow wrote: 'I sometimes think that the world will either be saved by psychologists – in the very broadest sense – or else it will not be saved at all.'[34]

It could be argued that Jungian psychology may be the main offender. It has been asserted that Jung had a messianic complex, and saw himself as the centre of a new form of religion which would arise, like a phoenix, from the ashes of a declining Christianity. Richard Noll has written a book entitled *The Jung Cult: The Origins of a Charismatic Movement*.[35] In it, he argues that Jung epitomised what Max Weber described as the prophetic charismatic leader. Weber said that the word 'prophet' should be understood to refer to a purely individual bearer of charisma, who by virtue of his or her mission proclaims a religious doctrine or what God desires. No radical distinction is made between a 'renewer of religion' who preaches an older revelation, and a 'founder of religion' who claims to bring a completely new message of deliverance. The two types merge into one another. According to Noll, Jung saw himself as such a prophet. He centered his disciples, mostly women, around himself. His new religion had its own distinctive notions of salvation and wholeness. It was individualistic, Gnostic, and critical of mainline Christianity.

---

33. *Dynamics of Faith* (New York: Harper & Row 1957), 83-85; *Psychology as Religion: The Cult of Self-worship* (Grand Rapids, Mich.: Eerdmans, 1980); G William Barnard, 'Diving into the Depths: Psychology as Religion' *Religion and Psychology: Mapping the Terrain* (London: Routledge, 2001) ed. Diane Jonte-Pace & William Parsons, 297-318.
34. Speech delivered at Nebraska Convention Jan 13th-14th 1955, quoted in *The Right to be Human: A Biography of Abraham Maslow* (Wellingborough: Crucible, 1989), 207.
35. (London: Fontana, 1996), 275.

While Jung's psychology contains some ideas that would not fit in with orthodox Christianity, e.g. that God is a quaternity rather than a trinity of persons, I don't think that Noll's iconoclastic criticism is justified. For example, speaking about the allegation that he was founding a new religion Jung said: 'If people have the peculiar impression that I preach a religion, this must be due to ignorance of psychotherapeutic methods.'[36] Speaking about the claim that he was re-founding Christianity from within, he said: 'I do not fiddle with dogma. In my eyes it has the highest authority, but I try to understand it, since unfortunately I cannot believe anything I do not understand, and in this I am like many other people today ... I have never anywhere denied God. I proceed from a positive Christianity, which is as much Catholic as it is Protestant ... Authors who take as positive a stand as I do in relation to Christianity deserve to be read more carefully and thoughtfully.'[37]

However, it can be said that, one way or the other, the New Age movement has adopted and adapted many of Jung's key ideas, such as the immanence of the divine in the self, and integrated them into its Gnostic enterprise, which advocates salvation, as wholeness and interconnectedness, as a result of higher, mystical states of consciousness.[38] They are brought about, in a Pelagian way, by means of one's own conscientious efforts which are sometimes referred to as psycho-technologies. As a recent document from the Vatican observed, the tendency to merge psychology and spirituality in this way was a characteristic of the Human Potential Movement as it developed towards the end of the 1960s at the Esalen Institute in California.[39] Transpersonal psychology, strongly influenced by Eastern reli-

---

36. *God and the Unconscious* (London: Fontana, 1964), 269
37. *God and the Unconscious*, op. cit., 271; 268.
38. Cf William Barnard, 'Diving into the Depths: Reflections on Psychology as Religion', *Religion and Psychology: Mapping the Terrain*, ed. Jonte-Pace & Parsons, op. cit., 297-318.
39. The Pontifical Council for Culture & The Pontifical Council for Inter-religious Dialogue, *Christ The Bearer of the Waters of Life: A Christian Reflection on the New Age.*

gions and by Jung, offers a contemplative journey where science meets mysticism. Stress is laid on the search for ways of expanding consciousness and the cultivation of the collective unconscious. To realise one's potential, one has to go beyond the ego in order to become the God that one is, deep down. This can be done by choosing the appropriate psycho-technology, whether meditation, para-psychological experiences, or the use of hallucinogenic drugs. These are all ways of achieving mystical fusion by means of 'peak experiences' with a pantheistic God who is present both within oneself and the cosmos.

Conclusion

The relationship between psychology and religion/spirituality is fraught with tensions. As we have seen, religion and spirituality are likely to be the victims. That said, psychology can throw a valuable light upon the nature and dynamics of human nature, the very nature that is perfected by the grace of God. The following chapters will explore some aspects of that relationship.

CHAPTER TWO

Transpersonal Psychology and Spirituality

It is said that there are four main branches on the tree of modern psychology. Firstly, there is psychoanalysis which studies the influence of the unconscious mind on conscious awareness and behaviour. Among its better known practitioners are Sigmund Freud, Alfred Adler, Erik Erikson, Carl Jung, Erich Fromm, Karen Horney, Otto Rank, Melanie Klein, and Harry Sullivan. Secondly, there is behaviorism which focuses on objectively observable behaviours while discounting mental activities. Among its principle proponents are Ivan Pavlov, John Watson and Burrhus Skinner. Thirdly, there is humanistic psychology, which is influenced by existentialist philosophy and highlights the human dimension of psychology. The names most associated with this type of psychology are Abraham Maslow, Carl Rogers, and Rollo May. Fourthly, there is transpersonal psychology which developed from humanistic psychology. It emphasises the importance of spirituality and transcendental experiences such mystical states of consciousness in a psychology that studies the whole of human experience.

The term 'transpersonal' denotes beyond the personal self or personal identity. Transpersonal experiences can be defined as those in which the sense of identity or self extends beyond the individual or personal to encompass wider aspects of humankind, life, psyche, and cosmos.[1] One general definition of transpersonal psychology is that it is concerned with the study of humanity's highest potential, and with the recognition, understanding, and realisation of unitive, spiritual, and transcendent states of con-

---

1. Walsh, R. & Vaughan, F. (eds) *Paths beyond ego: The Transpersonal Vision* (Los Angeles: J. P. Tarcher 1993), 3.

sciousness.[2] When *The Journal of Transpersonal Psychology* began publication in the late 1960s Anthony Sutich stated that transpersonal psychology included the empirical study of 'transpersonal process, values and states, unitive consciousness, meta-needs, peak-experiences, ecstasy, mystical experience, being, essence, bliss, awe, wonder, transcendence of self, spirit, sacralisation of everyday life, oneness, cosmic awareness, cosmic play, individual and species-wide synergy, the theories and practices of meditation, spiritual paths, compassion, transpersonal co-operation, transpersonal realisation and actualisation; and related concepts, experiences and activities.' While this paragraph would need unpacking, the general gist is clear. Transpersonal psychologists are at pains to point out that although their subject doesn't espouse any particular religious beliefs it does try to understand the universal human need that has led to the formation of different religions. Some of the names associated with this kind of psychology are William James, Carl Jung, Viktor Frankl, Abraham Maslow, Ken Wilber, Stanislav Grof, and Roberto Assagioli. This chapter will focus on this fourth kind of psychology by describing the contributions of some of the more notable names associated with it.

Richard Maurice Bucke

I suspect that the person who first explored the transpersonal or sacred aspects of psychology was a Canadian doctor named Richard Maurice Bucke (1837-1902). Shortly before his death he published a very interesting book entitled *Cosmic Consciousness: A Study in the Evolution of the Human Mind*.[3] Having explored the mental and spiritual activity of the human race, he suggested that more and more people were being graced by higher states of mystical consciousness. He noted that, typically, people like Moses, Gautama, Socrates, Jesus, Paul, and Plotinus experi-

---

2. Lajoie, D. H. & Shapiro, S. I. (1992), 'Definitions of transpersonal psychology: The first twenty-three years', *Journal of Transpersonal Psychology*, (Vol 24, 1992), 91.
3. (New York: Dutton, 1969)

enced this kind of inner illumination in their mid to late thirties. Bucke maintained that the exceptional people who undergo this experience know that the universe is a living presence, that life is eternal, the soul of humans is immortal, the foundational principle of life is love, and that the happiness of every individual is, in the long run, absolutely certain. As a result, all fear of death disappears, all anxious preoccupation with sin is lost, and the personality gains added charm and is transfigured. The individual learns more in a few moments of enlightenment than in long periods of study. Walt Whitman described cosmic consciousness as 'ineffable light, light rare, untellable, light beyond all signs, descriptions and languages,'[4] Having outlined the characteristics of cosmic consciousness, Bucke offered eighteen biographical examples of mystical illumination, including that of Whitman. He illustrated how, in each case, the enlightened individual conformed to the typical template of cosmic consciousness.

William James
William James (1842-1910) was a great admirer of Bucke's insights. In 1902, the year of Bucke's death, he published the text of his famous Gifford lectures, entitled, *The Varieties of Religious Experience: A Study in Human Nature.*[5] Writing about his objective he said: 'The problem I have set myself is a hard one: first, to defend ... 'experience' against 'philosophy' as being the real backbone of the world's religious life ... and second, to make the hearer or reader believe, what I myself invincibly do believe, that, although all the special manifestations of religion may have been absurd (I mean its creeds and theories), yet the life of it as a whole is mankind's most important function.'[6] James highlighted the importance of religious experience and maintained that it is from such experiences that theologies, philosophies and ecclesi-

---

4. 'Prayer of Columbus', *Leaves of Grass* (1900)
5. (London: Fontana, 1971)
6. Quoted by David Wulff, *Psychology of Religion: Classic and Contemporary Views* (New York: Wiley 1997), 475.

astical organisations may secondarily grow. As a result, he felt that churches played a secondary role in transmitting their originating inspiration. It is also clear he regarded popular piety as something inferior and second hand.

In lectures four to seven, James made a distinction between the healthy minded or once-born, and the sick souled or twice-born religious person. As Wulff points out, 'Strictly speaking these two types represent, not religious varieties *per se*, but temperamental predispositions to perceive the world in different ways.'[7] People who are healthy minded tend to have a very positive outlook on life, they see everything as good, while being inclined to minimise the reality of evil. They have sunny, enthusiastic temperaments and, from a religious point of view, they have a spirit of grateful admiration and a desire for union with the divine. James cites Ralf Waldo Emerson and Walt Whitman as examples of this kind of outlook.

Sick-souled people, on the other hand, are painfully aware of evil in the world. They tend to be melancholic and fearful. They acknowledge that the evil they sense in the outer reality resonates within their own minds as well. No matter how neurotic they may be, sick souled people encompass this broader range of experience. James cited John Bunyan and Leo Tolstoy as examples of this type. He could also have cited himself. What shifts sick souled people to greater health is the experience of religious conversion. James stresses the role of the unconscious in the process. A possible example of this kind of radical change would be the account of Paul's experience on the road to Damascus. While it seemed without preceding cause, it could be argued that it was due to the fact that, unconsciously, he had realised that he was contending with a superior religious force, as epitomised by the holiness and courage of Stephen, the martyr. As Henri Troyat's magnificent biography also indicates, Leo Tolstoy was another example of a sick-souled person who

---

7. *Psychology of Religion*, op. cit., 485

experienced inner reconciliation as a result of a conversion type experience.[8]

Mysticism was also one of James's interests. He dealt with this subject in lectures sixteen and seventeen. While he didn't reduce religion to mysticism he did claim 'that personal religious experience has its root and centre in mystical states of consciousness.'[9] Instead of defining mystical states, he said that they have four identifiable characteristics:

- Ineffability. In other words they defy expression. They cannot be adequately conveyed in language. One is reminded of T. S. Eliot's verse: 'Words strain, crack and sometimes break, under the burden, under the tension, slip, slide, perish, decay with imprecision.'[10] James believed that unless the hearer has had a similar experience, the one talking will fail to convey what the felt experience was really like.

- Noetic quality. Besides being states of feeling, mystical states also seem to those who have them, to be states of knowledge also. They intuit depths of truth which cannot be accessed by rational, discursive thought, e.g. St Ignatius of Loyola's insight into the Trinity at Manresa. Ignatius said: 'It is not much knowledge that fills and satisfies the soul, but the intimate understanding and relish of the truth.'[11]

- Transiency. Mystical states cannot be sustained for long. At best they might last for up to a half an hour, and even less frequently for an hour. Once they are over, their intensity is hard to recapture in memory.

- Passivity. Although the person may be disposed to have a mystical experience, e.g. by developing a capacity of paying sustained attention, such experiences are gratuitous. One cannot psyche oneself into a mystical awareness. 'The wind,' as scripture says, 'blows where it wills' (Jn 3:8).

---

8. *Tolstoy* (London: Pelican, 1970)

9. *Psychology and Religion: Classic and Contemporary Views,* op. cit., 299.

10. 'Burnt Norton', *Four Quartets,* line 149, (London: Faber & Faber, 1964), 19.

11. Quoted, Margaret Hebblethwaite, *Finding God in All Things* (London: Fount, 1987), 49.

James said that when people have mystical experiences they have predictable effects.

1. Mystical states, when well developed, usually are, and have the right to be, absolutely authoritative over the individuals to whom they come.

2. No authority emanates from them which should make it a duty for those who stand outside of them to accept their revelations uncritically. It is interesting to note that although Marian apparitions where authoritative for the people who experienced them, e.g. the young people in Fatima and Medjugorje, Catholics are not obliged to accept the messages they convey.

3. They break down the authority of the non-mystical or rationalistic consciousness which is based upon the understanding and the senses alone. They show it to be only one kind of consciousness.

Besides looking at this topic James dealt with many others, such as saintliness. Although he wasn't very religious himself, his psychology was transpersonal in so far as it maintained that religious experience was mankind's most important function. He described its dynamics in an insightful, individualistic way, while stating that such experiences were the birthplace of religion in the form of doctrines, rituals, morals and traditions. We will see in chapter eight how the founders of Alcoholics Anonymous integrated some of James's insights with their distinctive spirituality.

Carl Jung

Carl Jung (1875-1961) also made a significant contribution to the growth of transpersonal psychology. Aniela Jaffe said of him: 'Fundamentally his entire work is to be understood as a psycho-religious statement, a progressive interpretation of the numinous by which man is consciously or unconsciously filled, surrounded and led.'[12] Indeed, in his earlier writings he used the phrase 'transpersonal unconscious' as a synonym for the 'collective unconscious.' In his Terry lectures on 'Psychology and

---

12. Ronald Hayman, *A Life of Jung* (London: Bloomsbury, 1999), 220.

Religion' given at Yale in 1937 he quoted a saying of Cicero: 'Religion is that which gives reverence and worship to some higher nature which is called divine.' He went on to echo William James's point of view when he said: 'I want to make it clear that by the term "religion" I do not mean a creed.' He proceeded to point out that every creed is originally based upon the experience of the divine; upon trust, loyalty, and confidence evoked by an experience of a numinous nature together with the change of consciousness that ensues. On another occasion he said: 'We might say then that the term "religion" designates the attitude peculiar to a consciousness which has been changed by experience of the *numinosum*', i.e. the divine.[13]

Jung insisted that he wasn't looking at religious beliefs as such, rather he was examining people's experiences of them. Speaking of his methodology he said that he approached psychological matters from a scientific and not from a theological standpoint. Inasmuch as religion had a very important psychological aspect, he dealt with that from a purely empirical point of view. He restricted himself to observation of phenomena and avoided any metaphysical or philosophical considerations. That said, he did not deny the validity of these considerations, e.g. doctrinal truths, but *qua* psychologist he couldn't claim to be competent to deal with them correctly. He said that from a psychological point of view people don't experience God, but rather the God image which mediates their sense of God. 'We know that the God-image plays a great role in psychology,' he said, 'but we cannot prove the physical existence of God. As a responsible scientist I am not going to preach my personal and subjective convictions which I cannot prove.'[14] Speaking about the God image he said that when he spoke about God he always meant the image man has made of him. But no one knows what God is really like, or he would be God himself. While Jung would acknowledge that many symbols could act as God images,

---

13. Michael Palmer, *Freud and Jung on Religion (London: Routledge, 1997)*, 138
14. *Freud and Jung on Religion*, op. cit., 124-125.

Christ was the God image *par excellance* for western culture. It has a unique ability to mediate the numinous presence of God to the self. What makes this possible is what Jung referred to as the God-archetype, i.e. a psychic capacity for religious experience.

Jung believed that by coming to know Christ, a person could experience his presence within his or her deepest self. He wrote: 'He is in us and we are in him. His kingdom is the pearl of great price, the treasure buried in the field, the grain of mustard seed which will become a great tree, and the heavenly city. As Christ is in us, so also is his heavenly kingdom. These few, familiar references should be sufficient to make the psychological position of the Christ symbol quite clear. Christ exemplifies the archetype of the self.'[15] Jung believed that as one related by faith to Christ, one experienced his presence within. Speaking about himself he said: 'Christ is in us, and we are in him! Why should the activity of God and the presence of the Son of Man within us not be real and observable? Every day I am thankful to God that I have been allowed to experience the reality of the Divine Image within me. Had this not been granted me, I should indeed have been a bitter enemy of Christianity, and of the church especially. But thanks to this act of grace, my life has meaning, and my inward eye has been opened to the beauty and greatness of dogma.'[16] When one reads Jung's religious writings carefully it becomes apparent that, although he was a great advocate of the immanence of the divine, because of his psychological empiricism and philosophical Kantianism, he had little or no apparent appreciation of the simultaneous transcendence of God.

Jung was accused of regarding the words self and God as interchangeable. He himself denied this. He wrote: 'The self can never take the place of God, although it may, perhaps be a receptacle for divine grace. Such regrettable misunderstandings are due to the assumption that I am an irreligious man who does not believe in God, and should be shown the road to faith ... How

---

15. *Collected Works*, IXII, 69-70. Quoted in John Welsh, *Spiritual Pilgrims: Carl Jung and Teresa of Avila*, (New York: Paulist Press, 1982), 192.
16. Letter dated 13 January, 1948, in *God and the Unconscious*, op. cit. 273.

could any sane man suppose he could displace God, or do anything whatever to him? I am not so mad that I could be suspected of intending to create a substitute for God. How could any man replace God?'[17]

Jung often talked about individuation as being the psychological goal of the self. He felt that it could not be realised without religious experience. The symbols of the self and God are symbols of unity. All representations of God and the self must therefore be regarded as symbols of psychic wholeness. Jung wrote: 'When as a psychologist I speak of God, I am speaking of a psychological image. Similarly, the self is a psychological image of human wholeness, and it is also something transcendental because it is indescribable and incomprehensible.'[18] Jung felt that Western rationalistic culture favoured left brain thinking, i.e. of the rational, objective variety, rather than right brain thinking, i.e. of the subjective, intuitive and affective kind. As the story at the beginning of the introduction to this book indicates, he felt that modern culture was also too extroverted, too fascinated by the external world. As a result, the religious instinct was distrusted and repressed much as sexuality had been in Victorian times. Consequently people were alienated from their deeper selves and God. In chapter nine we will see how the spirituality of St Vincent de Paul can be understood with the help of Jungian psychology, and in chapter four we will explore the way his insights influenced the spirituality of Alcoholics Anonymous.

Viktor Frankl

Viktor Frankl (1905-1997) was born in Austria. He went through an atheistic phase in his teenage years. Although there was a religious dimension to all his adult writings he was reluctant to say whether he was a believer or not. He explained: 'I do not allow myself to confess personally whether I'm religious or not.

---

17. *Freud and Jung on Religion*, op. cit., 152.
18. *Freud and Jung on Religion*, op. cit., 152.

I'm writing as a psychologist, I'm writing as a psychiatrist, I'm writing as a man of the medical faculty ... And that made the message more powerful because if you were identifiably religious, immediately people would say, "Oh well, he's that religious psychologist".'[19] Like Jung he said, 'I have devoted a substantial part of my literary work to the mutual boundaries between psychotherapy and theology.'[20] He reflected Jung's point of view when he said that psychology, as a secular practice, couldn't go beyond the bounds set by medical science. It could open the door to religion, but only the patient could decide whether he or she wanted to pass through that door. In other words, psychology can lead people to the spiritual water of life, but only they can make the decision to drink.

His doctorate in philosophy was entitled *The Unconscious God*. It maintained that there is an 'unconscious religiousness,' a 'latent relation to transcendence' inherent in all people. Thus the spiritual unconscious is also the 'transcendent unconscious' the object of which can be called God. Although Frankl valued religion much as Jung had done, he differed from the latter in a number of ways. He did not locate the human capacity for spirituality in a God archetype in the collective unconscious, but rather in the human spirit. Whereas Jung talked only of an immanent God who was discovered in the deeper self, Frankl said that God was transcendent also, the Mystery of Supermeaning beyond the self. On his 90th birthday, he said that he believed in this Supermeaning and went on to add, that Supermeaning was something paralleling a Superbeing, and this Superbeing could be called God.

Frankl married in 1942, but in September of that year, he, his wife, father, mother, and brother, were arrested and brought to the concentration camp at Theresienstadt in Bohemia. Frankl had written a manuscript during the war, entitled *Doctor of the Soul*. When he was moved some time later to Auschwitz, his

---

19. Interview with Matthew Scully on the occasion of his 90th birthday.
20. *Recollections: An Autobiography* (Cambridge, Mass.: Basic Books, 2000), 57.

manuscript was destroyed. He described this experience as the loss of his mental child. Finally, after many vicissitudes, he was liberated in April 1945. He returned to Vienna, only to discover that all of his loved ones, with the exception of Stella his sister, had died. Soon after his arrival he dictated his best known book over a period of nine days. In German it was entitled *Say Yes to Life in Spite of Everything* and in English *Man's Search for Meaning*. It is estimated that it has sold ten million copies since its publication.

According to Frankl people are not just determined by an unconscious instinctual element as Freud maintained, or an unconscious psychical element as Jung had implied, but by an unconscious spiritual element. Frankl defined spirituality as a desire or search for unconditional meaning. Our deepest desire, he maintained, is not for happiness, self-realisation, self-fulfillment, self-development or self-actualisation. It is through the self-transcending pursuit of meaning that these other desirable states can follow. Frankl believed that there were three main ways of discovering meaning:

1) Creativity, by giving something to the world through self-expression: using one's talents in various ways through the work we do, and the gifts we give to life.

2) Experiencing life through interaction with nature, culture, the environment, and other people, especially in loving relationships.

3) Changing attitudes. Even if one can't change a situation, one can still choose one's attitude toward it. This will often be a self-transcending way of finding meaning, especially in cases of unavoidable suffering.

Frankl believed that being human was always being orientated to something or someone other than oneself, e.g. a meaning to fulfill, a human being to encounter, a cause to serve, or a person to love. It was only to the extent that a person was living out of this self-transcendence of human existence that he or she was truly human or capable of becoming his or her true self. Frankl was convinced that neither psychosis nor repression was able to annul this capacity. It is always there in the background of consciousness.

In another of his essays, Frankl expanded upon this point. 'Man is responsible for the fulfillment of the specific meaning of his personal life,' he observed, 'but he is also responsible before something, or to something, be it society, or humanity, or mankind, or his own conscience. However, there is a significant number of people who interpret their own existence not just in terms of being responsible to something but rather to someone, namely to God.'[21] Frankl often quoted a saying from Nietzsche which could have been a motto for his psychotherapeutic work in the concentration camp: 'He who knows a *why* for living, will surmount almost every *how*.'[22]

a) The Meaning of Love

Frankl maintained, that we find meaning, pre-eminently through love. He said that by means of love a person is 'enabled to see the essential traits and features in the beloved person; and even more, he sees that which is potential in him, which is not yet actualised but yet ought to be actualised.'[23] In *Man's Search for Meaning* there is one of the most beautiful passages about spiritual love that I have ever read, one which encapsulates what Frankl meant. He tells us that during a time when he was suffering extreme hardship in a concentration camp, he began to think about Tilly, his young wife, from whom he had been separated shortly after their marriage. 'My mind was on my wife's image,' he says, 'imagining it with an uncanny acuteness. I heard her answering me, saw her smile, her frank and encouraging look. Real or not her look was then more luminous than the sun which was beginning to rise. A thought transfixed me: for the first time in my life I saw the truth as it was set into song by so many poets, proclaimed as the final wisdom by so many thinkers. The

---

21. 'The Philosophical Foundations of Logotherapy,' *Psychotherapy and Existentialism* (London: Pelican, 1967), 23.
22. *Man's Search for Meaning* (New York: Washington Square Books, 1985), 97.
23. *Man's Search for Meaning*, op. cit., 134.

truth – that love is the ultimate and highest goal to which man can aspire. Then I grasped the meaning of the greatest secret that human poetry and human thought and belief have to impart: The salvation of man is through love and in love. I understood how a man who has nothing left in this world still may know bliss, be it only for a brief moment, in the contemplation of his beloved ... For the first time in my life I was able to understand the meaning of the words, "The angels are lost in perpetual contemplation of an infinite glory".'[24] A little later Frankl adds: 'Love goes far beyond the physical person of the beloved. It finds its deepest meaning in his spiritual being, his inner self. Whether or not he is actually present, whether or not he is still alive at all, ceases somehow to be of importance.'[25] Clearly, true companionate or romantic love can manifest the meaning of the God who is love

b) The Meaning of Suffering

Suffering comes to all of us, sooner or later. Not surprisingly, it was a central problem in the concentration camps where there was so much brutality, hunger, cold, disease and death. As the saying goes, suffering either makes a person bitter or better. It all depends on whether one can see meaning in it. In this connection, Frankl quoted a couple of lines from Wilde's *Ballad of Reading Gaol*: 'Nothing in the whole world is meaningless, suffering least of all.' In one of his writings he described how an important realisation came to him during his incarceration. He felt that it was likely that he would die in the near future. In this situation the question he asked himself was different from the one many of his comrades were asking. Their question was, 'will we survive the camp? For, if not, all this suffering has no meaning.' The question that beset Frankl was, 'Has all this suffering, this dying around us, a meaning?' For, if not, then ultimately there is no meaning to survival; for a life whose meaning depends upon such a happenstance – as whether one escapes or not – ultimately

---

24. *Man's Search for Meaning,* op., cit., 57.
25. *Man's Search for Meaning,* op. cit. 58.

would not be worth living at all.'[26] This is a profound point. Frankl believed that people need to go beyond conditional meaning to be motivated by unconditional meanings.

The doctor went on to say that he would like to clarify his views with an example. One day two prisoners sat before him. Both had resolved to commit suicide and used a phrase which was common in the camp: 'I have nothing more to expect of life.' He said that it was very important that the two men would undergo a Copernican revolution so that they would no longer ask what they could expect from life, but were made aware of the fact that life was awaiting something from them – that for each of them, indeed for all the prisoners, somebody or something was waiting, whether it was work to be done or an other human being. But what if this waiting should prove to be without prospect of fulfillment? Even then, said Frankl, somebody was invisibly present in the consciousness of every single prisoner, whether living or dead, but yet present and at hand. 'For many,' he said, 'it was the first, the last and ultimate Thou: God. But whoever occupied this position, the most important thing was to ask, What does he expect of me – that is, what kind of an attitude is required of me? So the ultimate matter was the way in which a person understood how to suffer, or to know how to die. This as we have been told is the quintessence of all philosophising.'[27]

c) Existential Frustration

Frankl believed that in modern secular culture many people are starved of the meanings he had discussed. That absence leads them to suffer from an emptiness at the centre of their lives, what he called existential frustration which often finds expression in boredom and angst. He said that it gave rise to Sunday neurosis, 'the kind of depression which afflicts people who be-

---

26. *Man's Search for Meaning*, op. cit., 138.
27. 'Group Psychotherapeutic Experiences in a Concentration Camp,' *Psychotherapy and Existentialism: Selected Papers on Logotherapy* op. cit., 102-103.

come aware of the lack of content in their lives when the rush of the busy week is over and the void within them becomes manifest.'[28] Frankl believed that existential frustration was the bitter fruit of a constricted, underdeveloped spirit which was starved of the oxygen of meaning. He wrote: 'This existential vacuum, along with other causes, can result in neurotic illness.'[29] Frankl also believed that when people suppressed their religious sense, their unfulfilled desire for meaning would be displaced into unhealthy attitudes and behaviours. They would end up making things like possessions, pleasure, power, and position into idolatrous substitutes for uncreated meaning.

Frankl believed that common problems in Western countries, such as depression, aggression and addiction, were often rooted in the experience of existential frustration. He explained: 'Sometimes the frustrated will to meaning is vicariously compensated for by a will to power, including the most primitive form of the will to power, the will to money. In other cases the place of the frustrated will to meaning is taken by the will to pleasure. That is why existential frustration often leads to sexual compensation. We can observe in such cases that the sexual libido becomes rampant in the existential vacuum.'[30] It is interesting to note that shortly before his death, Pope John Paul II seemed to echo Frankl's evaluation when he wrote in *The Church in Europe*: 'Among the troubling indications of the loss of a Christian memory are the inner emptiness that grips many people and the loss of meaning in life. The signs and fruits of this existential anguish include, in particular, the diminishing number of births, the decline in the number of vocations to the priesthood and religious life, and the difficulty, if not the outright refusal, to make lifelong commitments, including marriage. We find ourselves before a widespread existential fragmentation. A feeling of loneliness is prevalent; divisions and conflicts are on the rise.'[31] Of all

---

28. *Man's Search for Meaning*, op. cit., 129.
29. *Psychotherapy and Existentialism*, op. cit., 51.
30. *Man's Search For Meaning*, op. cit., 129-130.
31. Par 8.

the psychologists surveyed in this chapter, it is arguable that the transpersonal psychology of Viktor Frankl is the one with the greatest affinity with Christian spirituality.

Abraham Maslow

Speaking about his work American psychologist, Abraham Maslow (1908-1970) said: 'My goal is to integrate into a single theoretical structure the partial truths …in Freud, Adler, Jung … It is as if Freud supplied to us the sick half of psychology, and we must now fill out with the healthy half.'[32] Instead of studying neurotics as Freud and Jung had done, Maslow decided to study people who were very successful at living – he called them self-actualisers – in order to see what made them tick. 'Self-actualis-ation,' he wrote, 'may be loosely described as the full use and ex-ploitation of talents, capacities, potentialities, etc. Such people seem to be fulfilling themselves and to be doing the best that they are capable of doing, reminding us of Nietzsche's exhort-ation, "Become what you are".'[33] Maslow's thinking had affini-ties with Jung's because the notions of individuation and self-actualisation are quite similar.

Maslow found that people were motivated by a succession of hierarchically ordered needs:

1. Physiological needs such as food, drink, oxygen, rest, activity and sex.
2. Safety needs such as protection from dangerous people, ob-jects and situations in the form of things like the weather, ill-ness and the like.
3. Love and belongingness needs such a sense of love, accept-ance, affection and identification with a group/s.
4. Esteem needs in the form of competence at what one is doing and having the respect and goodwill of others.
5. Cognitive needs for knowledge and understanding, an ability

32. Richard Gross, *Psychology: The Science of Mind and Behaviour* (London: Hodder & Stoughton, 1992), 905.
33. Cf Jones & Crandall, 'Short index of Self-actualization Scale', *Measures of Religiosity*, eds. Hill & Hood (Birmingham, Alabama: Religious Education Press, 1999), 521-523.

to satisfy one's curiosity in such a way as to make sense of things.

6. Aesthetic needs such as beauty in art, symmetry in nature, balance, order and form in all things.
7. Self-actualisation needs, i.e. fulfilling one's full potential, everything one is capable of becoming.

This is quite a relevant schema in affluent countries, such as Ireland, because Maslow would argue that as people have their lower needs satisfied they tend to move on to satisfy the higher ones. Only a minority, however, would reach the self-actualisation stage. He found that self-actualisers were different from other people in a number of ways. Whereas most people tended to be self-centred, and mistrustful of threatening reality, self-actualisers were self-forgetful and open to the mystery of the world. Whether they were theists or atheists, said Maslow, self-actualised people were usually religious in the sense that they often reported having peak-experiences of a mystical kind.[34] He cited Marghanita Laski's book *Ecstasy* because it contained many examples of the kind of experiences he had in mind.[35] These epiphanies were triggered by such things as scenes of natural beauty, religious rituals, creative activity, scientific discovery, intellectual insight, sexual experience, childbirth etc. Maslow himself testified to the fact that he had enjoyed such experiences. For instance, speaking about a visit to Boston he said: 'The first time I saw the Charles river I almost died ... It was a very, very great experience, profoundly aesthetic ... I remember collapsing in a chair and looking at all this in just perfect wonder ... The place was so beautiful that it would crack your skull open, it was almost painful.'[36]

Commenting on the spiritual dimension of such experiences, Maslow wrote: 'A few centuries ago these would all have been described as men who walk in the path of God or as godly men.

---

34. Abraham Maslow, 'Religious Aspects of Religious Experiences', *Personality and Religion* (London: SCM, 1970), 168-179.
35. (London: Cresset, 1961).
36. Hoffman, *The Right to be Human*, op. cit., 267.

A few say that they believe in God, but describe this God more as a metaphysical concept than as a personal figure. If religion is defined only in socio-behavioural terms, then these are all religious people, the atheist included. But if more conservatively we use the term religion so as to include and stress the supernatural element and institutional orthodoxy then our answer must be quite different, for then almost none of them is religious.'[37] Maslow believed that genuine religious experiences could have a therapeutic effect. He wrote: 'The power of the peak-experience could permanently affect one's attitude toward life. A single glimpse of heaven is enough to confirm its existence even if it is never experienced again. It is my strong suspicion that one such experience might be able to prevent suicide, for instance, and perhaps, many varieties of low self-destruction, such as alcoholism, drug addiction and addiction to violence.'[38]

It is an ironic fact that, although Maslow was an atheist, he was aware of the sacred dimension of life. Like some other psychologists, already referred to, he believed that many people in contemporary society were repressing their sense of the holy. 'De-sacralising is a defence,' he observed, 'a flight from something, a fear of confrontation with, a fear of consciousness of the sacred.'[39] As a result of his emphasis on the sacred and the spiritual, Maslow's writings are described as transpersonal psychology.

Maslow's thinking about spirituality is similar to Jung's in so far as it says that people with integrated personalities are inclined to have peak-experiences of a religious kind. Such experiences are at once the cause and effect of integration. Maslow differs from Jung in so far as he refers to a more extroverted kind of contemplation of reality, whether one calls it the mystery of the universe or God. However, Maslow was mistaken in saying that self-actualisation is the ultimate motive of human life. This devalues the world of people and things. It turns them into a

37. *Motivation and Personality* (New York: Harper, 1970), 169.
38. Hoffman, *The Right to be Human*, op. cit., 277.
39. Cf Hoffman's *The Right to be Human*, op. cit., 278.

means to a desired personal end. He stated quite explicitly that: 'the environment is no more than a means to the person's self-actualising ends.'[40] Surely self-actualisation is an effect of self-transcendence rather than its chief aim.

While I think that there is some truth in what Jung and Maslow proposed in their psychologies, their findings about individuation and self-actualisation can be misleading. Both approaches tend to be elitist in so far as they seem to say that people are spiritual in so far as they are successful either in becoming individuated or self-actualised. In the Christian religion, however, grace is not necessarily associated with successful living. The good news of God's unconditional love is offered to the poor, outcasts, sinners, and failures; in other words to people who haven't got their act together. This implies that people who are either mentally handicapped or afflicted with a psychiatric problem can be holier than those who, although they are psychologically healthy by conventional standards, choose to lead immoral, unloving lives. In other words a person can be unwell or deficient at the level of the mind while being healthy at the level of the spirit. In common with New Age spirituality,[41] the psychology of Maslow seems to be Gnostic in so far as it stresses the importance of states of unitive consciousness rather than a good, benevolent will. New Age spirituality which borrows from Maslow, maintains that heightened states of consciousness can be achieved in a Pelagian way by means of one's own unaided efforts, whereas Christian holiness, as the choice to love in an unconditional way, can only be achieved through reliance on the free gift of God's Spirit.

Roberto Assagioli
This survey of transpersonal psychology is by no means complete. Not only is the description of each psychologist's thinking very brief, the work of many other transpersonal psychologists

---

40. *Motivation and Personality* (New York: Harper and Row, 1954), 117.
41. Cf Pat Collins, 'New Age Spirituality', *Spirituality for the 21st Century* (Dublin: Columba, 199), 106-113; 'The New Age Movement Evaluated' *He Has Anointed Me* (Luton: New Life, 2005), 154-159.

is not dealt with. That said, I'd like to mention two more, albeit briefly. Roberto Assagioli (1888-1974) was an Italian psychologist and the originator of psychosynthesis, i.e. an holistic theory that seeks to integrate body, mind, emotions and spirit, thereby making the individual into a balanced person. Psychosynthesis has a lot in common with Jungian psychology, but what is distinctive in it is the notion that besides the lower unconscious, which was explored by Freud and others, there is also a middle unconscious (similar to Jung's personal unconscious) and a higher unconscious, or superconscious which is an autonomous realm from which originate our more highly evolved impulses: altruistic love, humanitarian action, artistic and scientific inspiration, philosophic and spiritual insight, and the drive toward purpose and meaning in life. Psychosynthesis is concerned with integrating material from the lower unconscious and actualising the content of the superconscious. In one of his books *Transpersonal Development: The Dimension Beyond Psychosynthesis*[42] which was published posthumously, Assagioli deals with one spiritual topic after another. It is striking that this book of psychology has sections entitled, 'Spiritual Awakening' and 'Spirituality in Everyday Life.' While he doesn't promote any particular religious beliefs, he makes it clear that people cannot develop their full human potential unless they deepen their spiritual lives. As a psychologist he describes both the fruits of spiritual development and typical barriers to such development.

Ken Wilber

Ken Wilber, who was born in 1949, is a very influential American thinker. He is sometimes referred to as the Einstein of consciousness. He is a practising Buddhist who is attracted by the notion of the perennial philosophy. The term was first used by the German mathematician and philosopher Gottfried Leibniz to designate the common, eternal philosophy that underlies all religious movements, in particular the mystical streams within them. The term was later popularised by Aldous Huxley in his

42. (London: Crucible, 1991)

marvellous book *The Perennial Philosophy*.[43] George Bernard Shaw described the basic assumption of the perennial philosophy when he observed that 'There is only one religion, though there are a hundred versions of it.'

Ken Wilber believes that the perennial philosophy was also 'the psychology that finds in the soul something similar to, or even identical with, divine Reality.'[44] In his very first book, *The Spectrum of Consciousness*,[45] written when he was only in his twenties, Wilber tried to provide a perennial psychology by mapping different levels of consciousness, especially higher ones, which had been neglected by conventional psychology. He admires Jung for opening up knowledge of the unconscious in a deeper way than Freud. But he feels that Jung confused aspects of the personal unconscious with superconsciousness. We have already seen how Assagioli avoids that problem. In the first part of his book Wilber discusses how people become alienated as a result of dualistic thinking that separates the knowing subject from objective reality, thus creating a 'spectrum of consciousness.' Wilber describes six stages of consciousness ranging from basic oceanic consciousness, through the subtle stage described by parapsychology to the realm of supreme consciousness in the form of mysticism. The levels, he says, are structured in such a way that lower ones are integrated into the higher ones.[46] The second part of *The Spectrum of Consciousness* goes on to show that through growth and development, the dualistic fragmentation of the psyche may be overcome so that mystical wholeness is rediscovered. By surveying the traditions of the world's spiritual wisdom, Wilber attempts to unite modern psychology with spirituality, bringing the West and the East into harmony, since together they actually represent the perennial and universal psychology inherent in all human beings. Although many people

---

43. (London: Fontana, 1966)

44. *The Perennial Philosophy*, op. cit., 9.

45. (Wheaton: Quest Books, 1993)

46. Cf Bede Griffiths, 'The New Psychology and the Evolution of Consciousness', *A New Vision of Reality: Western Science, Eastern Mysticism and Christian Faith* (London: Collins, 1989), 28-56.

think that Wilber is a significant transpersonal psychologist, apparently the man himself has dissociated himself from that label.

Conclusion

When one reads through the literature of transpersonal psychology, it quickly becomes clear how perceptive and useful many of its insights are. Although this chapter has said very little about spirituality, it would be true to say that in the future spiritual writers will probably use many of its phenomenological descriptions when describing some of the subtle dynamics of mysticism. As was pointed out in the first chapter, although psychology is an empirical science, it can become a substitute spirituality of a Gnostic kind, like New Age spirituality. It has to be said that it is unlikely that any of the psychologists mentioned in this chapter intended their writings about the psychology of religious and spiritual consciousness to become religions or spiritualities in themselves. New Age spirituality, however, in its typically syncretistic way, has adopted a lot of ideas from transpersonal psychology. In times past it was said that philosophy was the handmaiden of theology. By analogy, it could be said that in our postmodern world transpersonal psychology can be the handmaiden, but not the mistress of a mature, self-aware spirituality.

CHAPTER THREE

Health, Happiness and Spirituality

Like many other religions, Christianity desires that its adherents would enjoy health and happiness. That was evident in the life and teachings of Jesus and his followers. When he was baptised, Jesus became consciously aware of the love of God in an unprecedented way. Speaking about this spiritual awakening in the life of Jesus, Pope Paul VI observed in his encyclical *On Christian Joy:* 'Jesus ... knows that he is loved by his Father. When he is baptised on the banks of the Jordan, this love, which is present from the first moment of his conception, is manifested. He knows that he is God's Son, the Beloved, who enjoys God's favour. This certitude is inseparable from the consciousness of Jesus. It is a presence which never leaves him all alone. It is an intimate knowledge which fills him ... For Jesus it is not a question of a passing awareness. It is the reverberation in his human consciousness of the love that he has always known as God in the bosom of the Father.'

As a result of his baptism, Jesus not only knew that he was the promised Messiah, he was also aware that God wanted him to proclaim the good news to the poor by loving them in the way that he was being loved by God. So following his baptism in the Jordan, Jesus did two main things. He preached the good news of God's incomprehensible love, especially to the poor. Rather than being under a curse, because of ignorance and a lack of good works, (cf Jn 7:49), they were under a torrent of God's unconditional and unrestricted mercy and love (cf Mt 5:3). He told them that he wanted their happiness. 'I have come that they may have life, and have it to the full', he declared (Jn 10:10). On another occasion he said: 'I have told you this so that my joy may

be in you and that your joy may be complete' (Jn 15:11). As St
Thomas Aquinas pointed out, 'Happiness is another name for
God. God is happy by nature; he does not attain happiness or receive it from another. But men become happy by receiving a
share in God's happiness, something God creates in them.'[1]

Jesus manifested the reality of that good news in three main
ways. Firstly, he related to the people in a compassionate, understanding manner which was devoid of judgement or condemnation. Secondly, he longed for their liberation from the unjust structures of religion and state. Thirdly, he performed deeds
of power such as healings, exorcisms and miracles. These signs
and wonders were the good news in action, supernatural indications of God's redeeming and liberating presence and power. It
is significant from a linguistic and theological point of view that
in the Greek of the New Testament the word *sozo*, which is derived from *saos* meaning 'to save,' also has the meaning 'to keep
in good health, to conserve, and preserve'.[2] It is worth recalling,
in this context that, when St John the Baptist was in prison he
sent messengers to ask Jesus whether he was the promised messiah. Jesus pointed to his proclamation and demonstration of the
good news: 'Go back,' he said, 'and report to John what you hear
and see: the blind receive sight, the lame walk, those who have
leprosy are cured, the deaf hear, the dead are raised, and the
good news is preached to the poor' (Mt 11:4-5).

The Commission to Proclaim and Demonstrate the Good News
During his lifetime Jesus instructed the apostles to participate in
his mission of increasing health and happiness by evangelising
in the way that he had done. Like him, they were to proclaim
and demonstrate the coming of the kingdom of God. For example, in Lk 9:1-2 we read: 'And he called the twelve together and
gave them power and authority over all demons and to cure dis-

---

1. *Summa Theologiae: A Concise Translation*, ed. Timothy Mc Dermott
(London: Methuen, 1989), 176.
2. Cf Leon-Dufour, *Dictionary of the New Testament* (San Francisco:
Harper & Row, 1980), 361.

eases, and he sent them out to preach the kingdom of God and to heal.' Before his ascension into heaven, the Lord commissioned the apostles to continue to do the same in the future. In Mk 16:15-19 we read: 'He said to them, "Go into all the world and preach the good news to all creation. Whoever believes and is baptised will be saved, but whoever does not believe will be condemned. And these signs will accompany those who believe: in my name they will drive out demons; they will speak in new tongues; they will pick up snakes with their hands; and when they drink deadly poison, it will not hurt them at all; they will place their hands on sick people, and they will get well".' There is clear evidence in the Acts, that the apostles carried out the Lord's instructions. They did 'the greater things' promised by Jesus in Jn 14:12. They not only proclaimed the good news in words, they demonstrated it in deeds. As Acts 2:43 testifies, 'Many wonders and signs were done through the apostles.'

St Paul provides us with an insight into the New Testament church's understanding of the gifts of power. He suggested that there were three interrelated kinds of gifts. Firstly, there were charisms of *revelation*, such as wisdom, knowledge and discernment which enabled people to understand the gospel. Secondly, there were charisms of *proclamation*, such as preaching, teaching and prophetic utterances, which enabled men and women to tell others about the good news. Thirdly, there were charisms of *demonstration*, such as healings – which included deliverance from evil spirits and miracle working. Paul says in 1 Cor 12:7 that the gifts, such as healings, are *phanerosis*, i.e. epiphanies that manifest the advent of God's kingdom of righteousness, joy and peace in the Holy Spirit.

It is interesting to see how St Paul clearly linked the gift of healing with effective evangelisation, especially in the ministries of apostles and evangelists. Speaking about himself, he said: 'For I will not dare to speak of anything except what Christ has accomplished through me to lead the Gentiles to obedience by word and deed, by the power of signs and wonders, by the power of the Spirit' (Rom 15:18-19). On another occasion he said:

'For we know, brothers loved by God, that he has chosen you, because our gospel came to you not simply with words, but also with power, with the Holy Spirit and with deep conviction' (1 Thess 1:4-5). On yet another occasion he said in similar vein: 'My message and my preaching were not with wise and persuasive words, but with a demonstration of the Spirit's power, so that your faith might not rest on men's wisdom, but on God's power' (1 Cor 2:4-5). Principal among the signs and wonders performed by Paul was healing. In Acts 28:7-9 we are told that having healed Publius and his ailing father on the island of Malta, Paul healed any of the sick who were brought to him. St Thomas Aquinas said perceptively that the confirmation of what is above reason, i.e. the core truths of Christianity, rests on the exercise of divine power.[3]

Healing in the Early Church

There is clear evidence that the charism of healing was exercised by many eminent Christians in the early centuries of Christianity.[4] Let me quote just two of the many extant examples. In the second century St Irenaeus wrote: 'For some do certainly and truly drive out devils, so that those who have thus been cleansed from evil spirits frequently join themselves to the church. Others have foreknowledge of things to come: they see visions, and utter prophecies. Others still, heal the sick by laying their hands upon them, and they are made whole … And what more shall I say? It is not possible to name the number of the gifts which the church throughout the whole world, has received from God, in the name of Jesus Christ.' In the fourth century St Hilary wrote in a commentary on Ps 64: 'We who are

---

3. St Thomas Aquinas, *Summa Theologiae: A Concise Translation,* ed. Timothy Mc Dermott (London: Methuen, 1989), 449; Commentary in 1 Cor 12:8-10, *Thomas Aquinas The Gifts of the Spirit: Selected Spiritual Writings (Chiefly from his biblical commentaries),* ed. Benedict Ashley, (New York: New City Press, 1995), 57-58.
4. Cf 'Signs and Wonders', *The New International Dictionary of the Pentecostal and Charismatic Movements,* eds. Burgess & Van Der Mass (Grand Rapids: Zondervan, 2002), 1063-1068.

reborn through the sacrament of baptism have the greatest joy, as we perceive within us the first stirrings of the Holy Spirit, as we begin to understand mysteries; we gain full knowledge of prophecy, speech full of wisdom, security in our hope, and gifts of healing and dominion over devils who are made subject to us.' In a book entitled, *Christianizing the Roman Empire*, Ramsay Mac Mullen, a professor of history and classics at Yale University has written: 'When careful assessment is made of passages in the ancient written evidence that clearly indicate a motive leading a person to conversion, they show (so far as I can discover): first, the operation of a desire for blessings ... second, and much more attested, a fear of physical pain ... third, and most frequent, credence in miracles.'[5] Apparently, what most impressed the people, especially the poor and uneducated of the time, were healings and exorcisms.

The Decline and Re-emergence of Christian Healing

One of the mysteries of the early church is the fact that the exercise of the charisms, including signs and wonders, had died out by the fifth century when Christianity became the official religion of the Roman Empire. For example, St John Chrysostom wrote at the end of the fourth century: 'The whole passage in 1 Cor 12:8-12, is very obscure, *but our ignorance is produced by our ignorance of the facts referred to,* (my italics) and by their cessation, being such as then used to occur, but no longer occur.' Why this happened is not entirely clear.

One explanation is what is known as the cessationist theory. It maintains, that once the early church was up and running with a hierarchy, sacraments and diocesan structures, the charisms were withdrawn. It quotes Eph 2:20 which says that the church 'is built upon the foundation of the apostles and prophets, with Christ Jesus as the cornerstone' in support of its belief. In other words, when the founders died, so did the signs and wonders. In the fourth century St Augustine adopted this point of view for a while. He wrote: 'Miracles are not allowed to continue into our

5. (New Haven: Yale University Press, 1984), 108.

time, lest the soul should always require things that can be seen, and by becoming accustomed to them mankind should grow cold towards the very thing whose novelty had made men glow with fire.'[6] It should be appreciated, however, that Augustine changed his mind in his *Refutations*, which was written later in his life. Having quoted what he had written earlier, he said: 'What I said should not be taken as understanding that no miracles are believed to happen today in the name of Christ.'[7] One of the reasons he said this was the fact that he had verified that many healings had taken place in his diocese, especially when people venerated the relics of St Stephen the martyr in St Augustine's church in Hippo.[8] In spite of what the saintly bishop said, the cessationist view became widespread, not only among Catholics but later among Protestants. Calvin wrote: 'The gift of healing, like the rest of the miracles, which the Lord willed to be brought forth for a time, has vanished away in order to make the new preaching of the gospel marvellous forever.'[9] In the nineteenth century John Nelson Darby put forward the dispensationalist theory which is similar to the cessationist one. It claims that church history is divided into eras or dispensations. For Darby the charismatic, apostolic, era was unique.

The rise of Newtonian and Cartesian science and the notion of the closed universe also had a detrimental effect. As David Hume and others tried to show, miracles are *a priori* impossible. For instance, in his *Enquiry Concerning Human Understanding*, 1748, Hume wrote: 'The many instances of forged miracles, and prophecies, and supernatural events, which, in all ages, have either been detected by contrary evidence, or which detect themselves by their absurdity, prove sufficiently the strong propensity of mankind to the extraordinary and marvellous, and ought reasonably to beget a suspicion against all relations of this kind.' Rudolf Bultmann, possibly the most influential scrip-

---

6. *De Vera Religione*, cap 25, nn 46, 47.
7. Cf Morton Kelsey, *Healing & Christianity*, (London: SCM, 1973), 185.
8. *Healing and Christianity*, op. cit., 185-186.
9. *Institutes*, Battle translation, 1960, p 1467.

ture scholar of the twentieth century, shared this naturalistic worldview. As a result he maintained that stories recounting signs and wonders, including exorcism and healing, should be demythologised. In his extended essay *Mythology and the New Testament* Bultmann wrote: 'Man's knowledge and mastery of the world have advanced to such an extent through science and technology that it is no longer possible for anyone seriously to hold the New Testament view of the world.'[10]

These are questionable points of view for a number of reasons. Firstly, they don't conform to the word of God. One could imagine Jesus saying to modern skeptics, what he once said to the Pharisees: 'You are in error because you do not know the scriptures or the power of God' (Mt 22:30). Secondly, down the ages there have always been saints who have either encouraged or exercised the gift of healing. For example, St Gregory of Palmas in the fourteenth century emphasised the laying on of hands for reception of healing and miracles. Saintly people such as Vincent Ferrer, Francis of Paola, Anthony of Padua and many others, performed deeds of power such as healing. Thirdly, the advent of the Pentecostal and Charismatic movements, together with the healing ministries of people such as Smith Wigglesworth,[11] Kathryn Kuhlman,[12] Agnes Sanford,[13] and Briege Mc Kenna[14] disproved the cessationist, dispensationalist and reductionist theories. Nowadays, official Catholic teaching accepts that the charism of healing is being exercised once again. For instance, besides taking it for granted that charismatic heal-

---

10. (London: SPCK, 1953); http://www.religion-online.org/indexby author.asp

11. Jack Hywel-Davies, *Baptized by Fire: The Story of Smith Wigglesworth* (London: Hodder & Stoughton, 2001); Smith Wigglesworth, *Greater Works: Experiencing God's Power* (New Kensington: Whitaker House, 1999)

12. Wayne Warner, *Kathryn Kuhlman: The Woman behind the Miracles* (Ann Arbor: Servant, 1993); Jamie Buckingham, *Daughter of Destiny* (Gainesville, Florida: Bridge-Logos, 2004); Kathryn Kuhlman, *I Believe in Miracles* (London: Lakeland, 1974).

13. Agnes Sanford, *The Healing Light* (Evesham: Arthur James, 1974)

14. Briege Mc Kenna, *Miracles Do Happen* (Dublin: Veritas, 1987).

ing is occurring in the church,[15] Pope Benedict has written: 'In the heart of a world adversely affected by rationalistic skepticism, a new experience of the Holy Spirit has come about, amounting to a worldwide renewal movement. What the New Testament describes with reference to the charisms as visible signs of the coming of the Spirit is no longer merely ancient, past history: this history is becoming a burning reality today.'[16]

It is worth noting that healing has also been associated with shrines like Lourdes. Its medical bureau applies criteria which were established in the 1700s by Pope Benedict XIV. He stipulated that in order to declare that a healing was miraculous it must be established that the disease was serious; that there was objective proof of its existence; that other treatments had failed; and that the cure was rapid, lasting and inexplicable from a scientific point of view.[17]

The case of Gabriel Gargam is probably one of the best known of the cures at Lourdes. In December of 1899 a train on which he was travelling collided with another train. Gargam was thrown fifty two feet from his carriage. He was paralysed from the waist down. After eight months he had wasted away to a mere skeleton, weighing only seventy-eight pounds. His feet became gangrenous. He could take no solid food and was obliged to take nourishment by a tube. He was brought to Lourdes. He was carried to the pool and placed in its waters. The exertion caused him to collapse and he seemed to be dead. As the priest passed by with the monstrance, he pronounced a blessing over the covered body. Soon, there was a movement from under the covering. To the amazement of the bystanders, the body raised

---

15. *Instruction on Prayers for Healing,* Sept. 14th 2000. Art 1 of the Disciplinary Norms says: 'It is licit for every member of the faithful to pray to God for healing. When this is organised in a church or other sacred place, it is appropriate that such prayers be led by an ordained minister.'

16. *Let God's Light Shine Forth: The Spiritual Vision of Benedict XVI* (London: Hutchinson, 2005), 101-102.

17. Renee Haynes, *Philosopher King: The Humanist Pope Benedict XIV* (London: Weidenfeld & Nicolson, 1970), 123-128.

itself to a sitting posture. While the family were looking on dumbfounded and the spectators gazed in amazement, Gargam said in a full, strong voice that he wanted to get up. They thought that it was a delirium before death, and tried to soothe him, but he was not to be restrained. He got up and stood erect, walked a few paces and said that he was cured. On 20 August, 1901, sixty prominent doctors examined Gargam and pronounced him entirely cured.

Holistic Healing and Psychology
As the preceding survey indicates, Christianity seeks to foster health and happiness not only by establishing and administering all kinds of medical facilities, but also by means of preaching the good news, administering its sacraments, many of which have a healing dimension, especially the eucharist, reconciliation and the anointing of the sick, and praying for healing. Nowadays, many Christian people approach the healing ministry with the help of psychology. Christians involved in inner healing and the healing of memories use many of the insights of modern psychologists in their work.[18] This fact is evident in books Charismatic healers have written about inner healing. They have borrowed, in an eclectic way, from different schools of psychology. For example, in *Healing Life's Hurts: Healing Memories Through the Five Stages of Forgiveness* the Linn brothers use Dr Kübler-Ross's research into the stages of death and dying.[19] In a later book, *Healing the Eight Stages of Life*, the Linn brothers and Sheila Fabricant use the psychosocial psychology of Erik Erickson as a framework for their discussion of inner healing.[20] In her classic book, *The Healing Light*, Agnes Sanford puts a lot of emphasis on the role of the unconscious mind.

Contemporary Christian healers are well aware of psychosomatic medicine. For instance, they are conscious that the medical profession maintains that prolonged periods of unhealthy

18. Cf John Shea 'Spirituality, Psychology and Psychotherapy', *The New SCM Dictionary of Christian Spirituality* (London: SCM, 2005), 49-54.
19. (New York: Paulist Press, 1978).
20. (New York: Paulist Press, 1988).

stress can have detrimental health effects, of a direct or an indirect kind. Up to 80% of all illnesses may be stress related.
Spiritual writers argue that if the mind influences the body,
surely the human spirit can influence mind and body, either for
good or ill. George Montague, a noted scripture scholar, has
written: 'If the *psyche* has such an influence on the body, might
not the spirit in turn have a powerful influence on the *psyche* and
through the *psyche* on the body as well? If we can speak of
psychosomatic diseases, might we not also speak of pneuma-
psychosomatic diseases? Such diseases have psychic and somatic
effects but their roots are really in the underdeveloped or constricted pneuma.'[21] There is a growing body of empirical evidence which suggests that Montague's hypothesis is correct.
Whereas the role of the mind on the body has long been ac-
knowledged, now the role of the human spirit in health is also
being accepted.[22] When we examined the writings of transpersonal psychologists such as Jung, Frankl and Maslow, we saw
that they believed that spiritual poverty, such as a lack of numinous experience (Jung), a sense of unconditional meaning
(Frankl), or peak-experiences of a mystical nature (Maslow),
could have detrimental psycho-somatic effects, e.g. high blood
pressure. The chapter on Alcoholics Anonymous makes it clear
that psycho-physical addiction to drink can best be overcome
through a spiritual awakening.

Psychology on the link between Spirituality and Healing
At this point we switch our perspective. Instead of looking at
what Christian spirituality says about health and happiness, we
will look at these topics from the point of view of psychology.
The theory of Christianity is one thing, the practice is another.
For example, in 1986 a French film, called *Thérèse*, was released.
It starred Catherine Mouchet and depicted the life of St Thérèse
of Lisieux as a devout, well intentioned young woman who was

---

21. Montague, *Riding the Wind*, op. cit., 36.
22. Pat Collins, 'Is Prayer Good for your Health?', *The Broken Image*
(Dublin: Columba, 2002).

living in a community of dysfunctional Carmelites. Her physical tuberculosis seemed to be a metaphor for the psycho-spiritual sickness that afflicted many, if not most of her companions. If one were to see the convent as a microcosm of Catholicism, the film seemed to be saying that a lot of religion is a sickness that mistakes itself for a cure. I have long suspected that there is some truth in this contention.

Psychology shows that many Christians fail to live up to the teachings of Christ. For instance some religious people, especially those who have fundamentalist views, tend to be more prejudiced than non-religious people.[23] Due to the strict sexual teachings of Catholicism, where every thought, word or deed contrary to the sixth commandment was said to be gravely sinful and deserving of eternal punishment, many Catholics have suffered from scrupulosity and neurotic forms of shame and guilt.[24] Freud's writings on the effects of the unhealthy super-ego explain the dynamics and effects of a good deal of this warped attitude which causes such unhappiness and misery. Catholic priests, among others, are all too well aware that, like themselves, many of the faithful can be surprisingly self-absorbed and delusional. I have often wondered whether people are emotionally dysfunctional because they are religious, or whether they espouse a warped form of religion because they are emotionally dysfunctional.[25] It is arguable that psychology, which focuses on religious experience rather than religious beliefs, has helped to answer this question and show that all that glitters in religion is not necessarily gold. It has helped to purify Christian spirituality by separating the dross of unconscious influences and attitudes, of an unhealthy kind, from the precious metal of genuine compassion and belief. For instance, it has helped to show how negative images of God, which were formed in childhood, can explain

---

23. Michael Argyle, *Psychology and Religion: An Introduction*, (London: Routledge, 2000), 194.
24. *Psychology and Religion: An Introduction*, op. cit., 175.
25. Cf Hood, Spilka, Hunsberger, & Gorush, 'Religion and Mental Disorder', *The Psychology of Religion: An Empirical Approach* (New York: The Guildford Press, 1996), 406-442.

why some people find it hard to pray. In their conscious minds they may believe that God is loving and benevolent, whereas in their unconscious minds they feel that God is distant, hard to please and punitive. Because their relationship with God is motivated more by conscious or unconscious fear than love, they avoid intimate relationship with the deity.

In recent years psychology has also tried to establish whether religion and spirituality are good for people's health and happiness. Levin and Schiller reviewed over 200 studies that related to this topic and concluded that they tend to go together.[26] In a more recent study of the same kind, Koenig, Mc Cullagh and Larson, concluded, 'There is ample evidence to demonstrate that religious belief and practice are associated with positive health behaviours.'[27] These general conclusions can be looked at a little more closely from a number of different points of view.

a) Advantages of Religious Practice
Religion and regular church attendance tend to improve health because practising Christians get support from other members of the community and because churchgoers are inclined to have healthier lifestyles. They tend to smoke less, have lower alcohol intake, better diets and avoid risky sex. Furthermore, it is quite likely that people with genuine spirituality will be more at peace and therefore less stressful. There is clear evidence that if these practices are motivated by faith there is a 25-33% less risk of premature death. Between the years 1987 and 1995 Hummer et al, conducted a random survey of 21,204 adults in the USA. They found that the average age of death for non-churchgoers was 75.3 years as compared to 81.9 years for churchgoers. This age advantage was particularly obvious in the case of women and Afro Americans.

---

26. *The Psychology of Religion: An Empirical Approach*, op. cit., 392.
27. David Fontana, 'Religion, Health and Well-Being', *Psychology, Religion, and Spirituality* (Oxford: Blackwell, 2003), 206.

b) Prayer and Health

Gordon Allport made a well known distinction between extrinsic and intrinsic religion. It can be noted in passing that St Paul makes a similar type distinction when he says: 'I gave you milk , not solid food, for you were not yet ready for it ... Anyone who lives on milk, being still an infant, is not acquainted with the teaching about righteousness. But solid food is for the mature, who by constant use have trained themselves to distinguish good from evil' (1 Cor 3:2; Heb 5:13-14). Those who espouse extrinsic religion: 'are disposed to use religion for their own ends ... Persons with this orientation may find religion useful in a variety of ways – to provide security and solace, sociability and distraction, status and self justification. The embraced creed is lightly held or else selectively shaped to fit more primary needs. In theological terms the extrinsic type turns to God, but without turning away from self.'[28] Typical examples of extrinsic religion would be: 'One reason for my being a church member is that such membership helps to establish a person in the community,' or 'The primary purpose of prayer is to gain relief and protection.' By and large, the prayer life of people who espouse this kind of sociological religion focuses on what God can do for them as opposed to who God is, or what they can do for God. As a result, they often split prayer from life. What they believe doesn't necessarily impinge upon the way in which they live. They tend to re-write the commandments, e.g. in business matters and sexuality, to suit themselves. If others object, they say, 'everybody is doing the same'. If and when religion and God seem to fail to meet their needs, they are like the people who found it hard to accept the teaching of Jesus on the eucharist, 'Because of this many of his disciples turned back and no longer went with him' (Jn 6:66).

Allport says that those who espouse intrinsic religion: 'find their master motive in religion. Other needs, strong as they may be, are regarded as of less ultimate significance, and they are, as

28. Allport and Ross 'Personal Religious Orientation and Prejudice', *Journal of Personality and Social Psychology*, no 5, pp 432-443.

far as possible, brought into harmony with the religious beliefs and preoccupations. Having embraced a creed, the individual endeavours to internalise it and follow it fully. It is in this sense that he lives his religion.'[29] Typical examples of intrinsic religion would be: 'It is important for me to spend periods of time in private religious thought and meditation,' or 'My religious beliefs are what really lie behind my whole approach to life.' People with mature, intrinsic religion are usually those who, as a result of a religious awakening and deep personal conviction, have committed their lives to God in a real, no strings attached, sort of way. The prayer life of the people who espouse this kind of religion focuses on knowing the person, word and will of God. Their growing relationship with the Lord tends to impinge more and more on the way they live. They are inclined to go against cultural trends by taking conscientious stands on all kinds of ethical issues, from honesty in business to purity of life. They are like the apostles, who although they found the teaching of Jesus on the eucharist hard to accept, responded to his query, 'Do you also wish to go away?' by saying, 'Lord to whom can we go? You have the words of eternal life' (Jn 6:67).

In an article entitled: 'Religious Orientation and Psychological Well-being: The Role of the Frequency of Personal Prayer,' which was published in *The British Journal of Health Psychology*, three researchers examined the effects of intrinsic religion on mental health. As has already been noted, people who have intrinsic, as opposed to extrinsic, religion are those who have internalised their faith in such a way that it influences every aspect of their everyday lives. Consequently, they are more inclined to have conscious awareness of the divine, and are more likely to have higher than average levels of self-esteem together with lower than average levels of anxiety and depression. These conclusions have been confirmed by a number of other studies.

---

29. Allport & Ross, *op. cit.*

c) Mystical Experience and Happiness

People with intrinsic faith are more inclined to have mystical type experiences of the extreme and mild kind described by James Pratt in his classic work. Both kinds report experiencing 'the sense of the presence of a being or reality through other means than the ordinary perceptive processes or reason.'[30] As was noted in the opening chapter, anything between 33 and 66% of the population in GB and the USA claim to have had such experiences. We noted in passing that many of them, especially in Britain, were not churchgoers. Apparently research in America has indicated that those who have had mystical type of experiences – they sound like Maslow's peak experiences – correlated positively with the Positive Affect Scale which is a good indicator of psychological well-being. They correlated in a negative way with the Negative Affect Scale, which is an indicator of poor mental health. As David Fontana says: 'overall the mystics emerged as notably happier and notably freer from mental disorders than the norm.'[31] Similar research which was conducted in England produced similar findings.

I have long admired the life and writings of Dom Bede Griffiths. Shortly before his death in May 1993 he suffered a stroke. Some time later he had a transforming mystical experience. Shirley Boulay described it in these words in *The Tablet:*[32]

> I had some breakfast and then I felt sort of restless, disturbed, not knowing quite what was happening. The inspiration came suddenly again to surrender to the Mother. It was quite unexpected: 'Surrender to the Mother.' And so I somehow made a surrender to the Mother. Then I had an experience of overwhelming love. Waves of love sort of flowed into me … I called out, 'I'm being overwhelmed by love.'
>
> The effects of this experience, of being totally engulfed in love, never left him. Always when talking about it he would

---

30. *The Religious Consciousness: A Psychological Study* (New York: McMillan, 1920), 337.
31. *Psychology, Religion and Spirituality*, op. cit., 217
32. 'Fr Bede's Breakthrough', *The Tablet* (12/09/1998).

stress that what he had felt as a blow on his head came from the left and propelled him towards the right, and this he interpreted as being a violent assertion of the feminine, the right side of the brain. At last, in his eighty-fourth year, he felt that 'the left brain and the whole rational system had been knocked down and the right brain and the intuitive understanding, the sympathetic mind, had been opened up'. And this was an experience of love.

Death, the Mother, the Void, was all love. It was an overwhelming love, so strong that I could not contain myself. I did not know whether I would survive. I knew 'I' had to die, but whether it would be in this world or another, I did not know. At first I thought I would die and just be engulfed in this love. It was the 'unconditional love' of which I had often spoken, utterly mysterious, beyond words.

So greatly did he feel himself loved, so awesome was this experience, that Bede wept during during the experience as he would sometimes weep, with happiness, when he recalled it. He knew that with this discovery of the feminine, he had been healed. The next afternoon he sprang out of bed and for the first time began to walk without his walking stick. This transpersonal experience was not only revelatory in a religious if not a specifically Christian way, it was an instance of the kind of pneuma-psychosomatic healing mentioned by George Montague.

d) Health Outcomes and Prayer for Others
Besides investigating whether prayer is good for personal health, researchers have also tried to establish whether prayer for others can have positive health effects. As I have dealt with this subject elsewhere I will not say too much about it here.[33] We will look at just one typical experiment. In 1988 a Dr Byrd of San Francisco General Hospital randomly divided a group of 393 coronary care patients into two groups, one of which was to receive prayers for healing plus medical help and the other which

---

33. Pat Collins, 'Is Prayer Good for your Health?', *The Broken Image*, op. cit., 86-92.

would receive medical help but no prayer. Over a ten month period, a panel of doctors assessed the patients for medical outcomes. When the results became available it was found that the people who had been prayed for, had done better than those who had not been prayed for. For example, while 3% of the people prayed with needed antibiotics, 16% of those who didn't receive prayer needed them. 6% of the people prayed for, developed fluid on the lungs, whereas 18% of those who were not prayed for did so. None of the people prayed for needed mechanical ventilation but 12% of the others did. Finally, and most importantly, 13% of the people prayed for died, and 17% of those not prayed for, passed away.

Dr Larry Dossey has indicated in a number of his books, e.g. *Prayer is Good Medicine*,[34] that there are many other studies which come to similar conclusions.[35] He cites the fact that currently, Dr Mitchell Krucoff at Duke University Medical Center, is studying the effects of prayer on patients undergoing cardiac procedures such as catheterisation and angioplasty. Those receiving prayer have up to 100% fewer side effects from these procedures than people not prayed for. These are double-blind studies, meaning that no one knows who is, or is not receiving prayer. This eliminates, or at least reduces, the influence of the placebo effect which is the power of suggestion and positive thinking. It would seem that intercessory prayer is good for the health of other people.

In view of all these points it is not surprising to hear that more and more medical schools, especially in the United States, are integrating spirituality into their courses. For instance, Duke University has established a Centre for the Study of Religion, Spirituality and Health. The fact that young doctors are now learning about these issues is an important indicator of impending developments. Indeed, it has even been suggested that, in the future, disappointed patients might take legal action against

34. (New York: Harper/Collins, 1997)
35. Cf http://www.godandscience.org/apologetics/religionhealth.html

those doctors who overlook the spiritual dimension of healing because research has indicated so clearly that it is important in any holistic notion of health. I suspect that the same trends could develop here in Europe.

Conclusion

In Christianity, the notions of salvation and healing are two sides of the same coin of divine grace. When it is at its best, Christianity promotes both in a way that increases human happiness. Although, there are defective forms of religion which do, undoubtedly, cause psychosomatic problems thereby decreasing health and happiness, there is a good deal of empirical evidence to show that those who are religious and have genuine spirituality are more inclined, on average, to be healthy in mind and body. As a result, they are more likely to be happy. In his book, *The Psychology of Happiness*, psychologist Michael Argyle says that 'religion is a definite though minor source of happiness, it is more important for old people, and is more strongly linked with marital happiness and health.'[36] Having stressed that genuine spirituality fosters health and happiness there is a danger that they would become ends in themselves. In reality they are the by-product of seeking meaning above all else. As Jesus said: 'Seek first God's kingdom and his righteousness, and all these things will be given to you as well' (Mt 6:33).

---

36. (London: Methuen, 1987), 125.

CHAPTER FOUR

Psychology and Spirituality in A.A.

Over the years I have discovered that spirituality and psychology came together in a very interesting way during the formation of Alcoholics Anonymous. This chapter will briefly recount the story of how this happened. Wherever possible, the words of the people directly and indirectly involved, will be quoted, namely recovering alcoholics Rowland Hazard, Edwin 'Ebby' Thacher, Bill Wilson, and Dr Bob Smith. Following that, the contribution of three eminent psychologists, William James, Carl Jung and Karen Horney to Alcoholics Anonymous will be assessed.

Rowland Hazard, a successful American business man, developed a very bad drink problem. For years he had floundered from one sanatorium to another. He had consulted the best known American psychiatrists[1] but without success. In 1931 he went to Zurich and was treated for the best part of a year by Carl Jung, the renowned Swiss psychologist. Rowland desperately wanted to get well and Jung did the best he could to help him.

Some years later Bill Wilson described Rowland's experience as follows: 'At the end of the year, feeling rather reassured that the world's greatest resource had been lavished on him, our friend left Dr Jung only to return in a short time in utter despair and in utter drunkenness. So he said to the doctor, "Well, what is there left?' And that very great man said to him, "I must confess, Rowland, that your case is of such a kind that I can't do anything about it. None of the resources that I command can expel this compulsion of yours to drink."

---

1. *The Big Book*, (New York: Alcoholics Anonymous World Services Inc, 2001), 26.

"Well," inquired Rowland, "Is this the end of the line?" And the doctor said, "No. There is one more resource and that is a conversion experience. I know you are already a man of faith and of belief, but I am talking about a transforming experience." "Well," said Rowland, "Where do I find such a thing?" The doctor responded, "Those things just happen. The lightning strikes on some people; on others it doesn't. You can't say in advance that anybody is going to have one, but you had better expose yourself to whatever religious resource you can and try to find such a thing".'[2]

Apparently, some time after this memorable meeting Rowland Hazard attended meetings of the Oxford Group, an evangelical fellowship, later known as Moral Disarmament. It stressed the importance of self-examination, confession, restitution, and the giving of oneself in service to others. Rowland was graced with a conversion type experience, stopped drinking, returned to the US and continued to attend Oxford Group meetings while trying to help fellow alcoholics. He met Edwin 'Ebby' Thacher, who, at that time, was facing a term of imprisonment as a consequence of his excessive drinking. When Rowland Hazard promised to take responsibility for him, Thacher was paroled into his care. Not surprisingly Hazard brought him to meetings of the Oxford Group in New York. Like his mentor, the latter was blessed, when he experienced a spiritual awakening, which empowered him to stop drinking.

Ebby Thacher was a friend of Bill Wilson, a New York stockbroker who, like himself, was a chronic alcoholic. Indeed one of his doctors had said to his wife Lois in 1934 that if he didn't stop drinking he would either go mad or die. Wilson himself admitted that: 'I had to be first in everything because in my perverse heart I felt myself the least of God's creatures.' Some years later Wilson recounted: 'Hearing of my plight, my friend Edwin Thacher came to see me at my home where I was drinking. By then, it was November 1934. I had long marked my friend Edwin for a hopeless case. Yet there he was in a very evident

---

2. Talk given in New York on Thurs March 25th 1954.

state of 'release' which could by no means be accounted for by his mere association, for a very short time, with the Oxford Groups. Yet this obvious state of release, as distinguished from his usual depression, was tremendously convincing. Because he was a kindred sufferer, he could unquestionably communicate with me at great depth. I knew at once I must find an experience like his, or die.'[3]

Sometime later while he was in hospital, Wilson cried out in utter despair, 'If there be a God, will he show himself?' This desperate desire was fulfilled when he had a quasi-mystical experience. He described it vividly in these words: 'Suddenly, my room blazed with an indescribable white light. I was seized with an ecstasy beyond description ... Then, seen in the mind's eye, there was a mountain. I stood upon its summit, where a great wind blew. A wind, not of air, but of spirit. In great, clean strength, it blew right through me. Then came the blazing thought, "You are a free man." ... a great peace stole over me ... I became acutely conscious of a Presence which seemed like a veritable sea of living spirit ... "This," I thought, "must be the great reality. The God of the preachers." I seemed to be possessed by the absolute, and the curious conviction deepened that no matter how wrong things seemed to be, there could be no question of the ultimate rightness of God's universe. For the first time I felt that I really belonged. I knew I was loved and could love in return.'[4]

Bill Wilson was 39 when he had that vivid religious experience. He never drank again. But he was tempted to do so soon afterwards. A few months following his encounter with the Higher Power he was in a hotel feeling lonely. Instead of taking a drink, however, he telephoned the director of a local church who told him about an alcoholic called Dr Bob Smith. Bill Wilson called to see him. That was the first ever AA meeting. They had discovered an important key to recovery. In giving

3. Letter of Bill Wilson to Carl Jung Jan 23rd 1961. It is mentioned in *The Big Book*, op. cit., 26-27, and in the Appendix below.
4. Bill Wilson, *Alcoholics Anonymous Comes of Age* (New York: Alcoholics Anonymous World Services, 1979), 121.

one receives (cf Lk 6:38; Acts 20:35). One holds on to one's own sobriety by helping another alcoholic to either attain or maintain his or her sobriety. Evidently, when two people share the same struggle they provide one another with a sense of belonging and help one another to get well.

In the wake of his dramatic conversion Bill Wilson conceived the idea of a society of alcoholics, where each member would transmit his or her experience to the next – chain style. If each sufferer were to point out, to prospective new members, the hopelessness of alcoholism from a scientific point of view, he or she might be able to alert the newcomers to the need to be open to an equally transforming spiritual experience. This concept proved to be the foundation of Alcoholics Anonymous' subsequent success. The famous twelve steps, which owed a lot to the disciplines of the Oxford Group, were formulated by Bill Wilson, with Dr Bob's help. Fr Ed Dowling, Wilson's Jesuit sponsor, pointed out that there were a number of similarities between the Twelve Steps and the Ignatian Exercises which Bill had read with great interest.[5]

Over the years, the 12 steps have been modified for use by such varied groups as Gamblers Anonymous, Cocaine Anonymous, Co-dependants Anonymous, Debtors Anonymous, Marijuana Anonymous, Overeaters Anonymous, Sex addicts Anonymous, Emotions Anonymous and Workaholics Anonymous. Here are the original 12 steps of A.A.:

1.   We admitted we were powerless over alcohol – that our lives had become unmanageable.
2.   Came to believe that a power greater than ourselves could restore us to sanity.
3.   Made a decision to turn our will and our lives over to the care of God as we understood him.
4.   Made a searching and fearless moral inventory of ourselves.
5.   Admitted to God, to ourselves, and to another human being the exact nature of our wrongs.

5. Robert Fitzgerald, 'The Spiritual Exercises and the Traditions', *The Soul of Sponsorship: The Friendship of Fr Ed Dowling SJ and Bill Wilson in Letters* (Center City, Minnesota, Hazelden, 1995), 58.

6. Were entirely ready to have God remove all these defects of character.
7. Humbly asked him to remove our shortcomings.
8. Made a list of all persons we had harmed, and became willing to make amends to them all.
9. Made direct amends to such people wherever possible, except when to do so would injure them or others.
10. Continued to take personal inventory and when we were wrong, promptly admitted it.
11. Sought though prayer and meditation to improve our conscious contact with God as we understood him, praying only for knowledge of his will for us and the power to carry that out.
12. Having had a spiritual awakening as the result of these steps, we tried to carry this message to alcoholics and to practise these principles in all our affairs.

It is arguable, that these transforming steps constitute one of the most significant contributions to spirituality in the twentieth century. Incidentally, Bill Wilson defined 'spirituality' as a reliance on our Creator. Dr Bob revealed in one of his talks that the principal ideas that influenced the spirituality of A. A. in the early days, came from the Bible, mainly 1 Corinthians 13, the Sermon on the Mount in Matthew, and the letter of James, whose practical approach was so influential that some early members wanted to call the A. A. fellowship 'the James Club'. The meetings held in Dr Bob's hometown of Akron, Ohio, between 1935 and 1939, were associated with the Oxford Group. The pioneers of that time went so far as to call themselves the 'Alcoholic Squad of the Oxford Group'. During the time members were in recovery, they usually had a quiet time each morning. It involved Bible study, prayer to God, listening for messages from God, and the use of helpful meditation literature. There were frequent discussions of every-day problems in the light of biblical teaching.

William James on Conversion

When one reads, Bill Wilson's accounts of the formation of A.A. it becomes clear that he was influenced by the writings of renowned American psychologist, William James, author of many books. Shortly following his conversion experience, his friend Edwin came to visit him in hospital. He gave him a copy of William James' *Varieties of Religious Experience* to read. The book argues, as we noted in chapter two, that there are sick-souled, once born individuals and healthy-minded twice born people. Conversion enables sick-souled people, in particular, to experience inner healing as a result of a reconciliation between the Dr Jeckel and Mr Hyde sides of the personality. We will examine how this happens in the section on Jung below. James described the dynamic in these words: 'To be converted is the process, gradual or sudden, by which a self hitherto divided, and consciously wrong, inferior and unhappy, becomes unified and consciously right, superior and happy, in consequence of its firmer hold upon religious realities.'[6] James stressed the role of the unconscious in all this. Things happen in the mind of the troubled person that s/he is not fully aware of. This is a kind of incubation period when the unconscious prepares the person for a sudden shift in consciousness. While psychology neither presupposes or requires that these forces transcend the individual, i.e. by means of the graceful activity of a Higher Power, Alcoholics Anonymous does. It could be argued that as grace builds on nature, psychology has discovered how it does so by means of the activity of the unconscious.

Describing his own story, Bill Wilson says that James's book gave him the realisation that most conversion experiences, whatever their variety, do have a common denominator, that of ego collapse at depth. In 1953 Wilson wrote that William James believed, 'Not only, could spiritual experiences make people saner, they could transform men and women so that they could do, feel and believe what had hitherto been impossible to them. It mattered little whether these awakenings were sudden or

---

6. *Varieties of Religious Experience* (London: Fontana, 1971), 194.

gradual, their variety could be almost infinite. But the biggest payoff of that noted book was this: in most of the cases described, those who had been transformed were hopeless people. In some controlling area of their lives they had met absolute defeat.'[7]

In Wilson's case defeat came in the form of his compulsive drinking and a deep feeling of hopelessness which had been heightened by his doctor. It was reinforced, still more, by his alcoholic friend, Rowland Hazard who said that neither medical or psychiatric help could effect a cure of his alcoholism. In his book *Will and Spirit: A Contemplative Psychology*, psychiatrist Gerald May says that transformation is a matter of moving away from the arbitrary control exercised by the willful ego, to the openness and receptivity of the willing self to centres of power and value beyond themselves. He describes the two dispositions in these words: 'Willingness implies a surrendering of one's self-separateness, an entering into, an immersion in the deepest processes of life itself. It is a realisation that one already is a part of some ultimate cosmic process and it is a commitment to participation in that process. In contrast, willfulness is the setting of oneself apart from the fundamental essence of life in an attempt to master, direct, control, or otherwise manipulate existence.'[8]

In appendix II of *The Big Book*, the official manual of Alcoholics Anonymous, we are told that the transforming movement from willfulness to willing openness to the higher power doesn't have to be dramatic like Bill Wilson's. *The Big Book* says: 'Most of our experiences are what the psychologist William James calls the "educational variety" because they develop slowly over a period of time. Quite often friends of the newcomer are aware of the difference long before he is himself. He finally realises that he has undergone a profound alteration in his reaction to life; that such a change could hardly have been brought about by himself alone. What often takes place in a few

---

7. 'A Fragment of History', *The Grapevine*, (July, 1953)
8. (San Francisco: Harper & Row, 1982), 6.

months could seldom have been accomplished by years of self-discipline.'[9]

Carl Jung on the Higher Power
It could be argued that William James exercised an indirect influence on the foundation of A.A. However, some twenty seven years after attaining his sobriety, Wilson wrote a very interesting letter to Carl Jung in mid January 1961.[10] As well as telling the well known doctor about his addiction and recovery he said: 'I doubt if you are aware that a certain conversation you once had with one of your patients, a Mr Rowland Hazard, back in the early 1930s, played a critical role in the founding of our Fellowship.' Wilson went on to add: 'Very many thoughtful members of A.A. are students of your writings. Because of your conviction that man is something more than intellect, emotion, and two dollars worth of chemicals, you have especially endeared yourself to us.'

A few days later Jung wrote a short, but fascinating, reply to Wilson. Referring to Rowland Hazard's excessive drinking, he said: 'His craving for alcohol was the equivalent, on a low level, of the spiritual thirst of our being for wholeness, expressed in medieval language: a desire for union with God.' To illustrate his meaning he quoted a verse of scripture: 'As the deer longs for flowing streams, so my soul longs for you, O God' (Ps 42:1). In other words, when people seek ecstatic happiness and a sense of belonging by drinking alcohol, they are looking for the right thing, in the wrong place. Later in the same letter Jung made the perceptive observation: 'You see, "alcohol" in Latin is "spiritus" and you use the same word for the highest religious experience as well as for the most depraving poison. The helpful formula therefore is: *spiritus contra spiritum*.' Put another way, a person will overcome addiction to spirits if, and when, he or she is filled with the Holy Spirit, i.e. the Higher Power.

It is worth noting in this regard, that William James had also

---

9. *The Big Book*, op. cit. 567.
10. cf Appendix, p 200.

highlighted the connection between drinking and religion when he wrote: 'The sway of alcohol over mankind is unquestionably due to its power to stimulate the mystical faculties of human nature, usually crushed to earth by the cold facts and dry criticisms of the sober hour ... The drunken consciousness is one bit of the mystic consciousness.'[11] Jung went on to say in his letter to Bill Wilson: 'The only right and legitimate way to such an experience (i.e. of the Higher Power) is that it happens to you *in reality* (my italics).' He said this, partly from personal experience. He wrote, 'Faith is a gift of grace if ever there was one, and I could never produce a gift of grace, however hard I tried.'[12] Jung went on to add that there are four possible ways in which religious experience could occur:

1) When you walk on a path which leads you to higher understanding.
2) You might be led to that goal by an act of grace.
3) It could happen through a personal and honest contact with friends.
4) It could happen through a higher education of the mind beyond the confines of mere rationalism.

As we saw in chapter two, Jung believed that people were likely to be neurotic without genuine religious experience.

In the light of Jung's letter to Bill Wilson and these quotes, it is evident why he was convinced that no neurotic ever recovered from his or her neurosis without having religious experience. As he said: 'In thirty years I have treated many patients in the second half of life.[13] Every one of them became ill because he or she had lost that which the living religions in every age have given their followers, (i.e. religious experience) and none of them was fully healed who did not regain his religious outlook.'[14] It is worth remembering that many of Jung's patients

---

11. *The Varieties of Religious Experience* (London: Fontana, 1971), 373.
12. Letter dated 13th Jan 1938, in Victor White, *God and the Unconscious* (London: Fontana, 1964), 271.
13. i.e. over 35 years of age.
14. 'Psychotherapists or The Clergy?', *Psychology and Western Religion* (London: Ark, 1988), 202.

were practising Christians, indeed, as we noted in the
Introduction, some of them were clergymen. He argued that
they got ill because, although they were committed to Christian
doctrines and rituals, they were starved of conscious experience
of God. As we saw in chapter two and three, other psychologists
have echoed Jung's point of view.

While Jung's letter to Wilson doesn't refer to James's belief
that religious conversion led to the reconciliation of the divided
self, this notion also played an important role in the Swiss doctor's psychology. He believed that neurosis, 'is an inner cleavage
– the state of being at war with oneself. Everything that accentu-
ates this cleavage makes the patient worse, and everything that
mitigates it tends to heal him. What drives people to war with
themselves is the suspicion that they consist of two persons in
opposition to one another. The conflict may be between the sen-
sual and the spiritual, between the ego and the shadow ...
Neurosis is a splitting of personality.'[15] Jung believed that one
part of the personality is lovable because it succeeds in living up
to its idealistic values and beliefs, while the other part, what he
called the shadow, is unlovable because it fails to do so. This is a
painful condition. Jesuit writer, John Powell has referred to it as
the 'toothache of the heart,' a chronic sense of emotional pain
that often leads people to use alcohol as an anesthetic. Jung
maintained that excessive drinking would not be overcome unless the person could deal with the basic cause, namely a lack of
self-acceptance. He observed in one of his most quoted sayings:
'Perhaps it sounds very simple, but simple things are always the
most difficult. In real life it requires the greatest discipline to be
simple, and the acceptance of oneself is the essence of the moral
problem and the epitome of a whole outlook upon life. That I
feed the hungry, forgive an insult and love my enemy in the
name of Christ – all these are undoubtedly great virtues. After
all, what I do for the least of my brothers and sisters, that I do to
Christ. But what if I discover that the least among them all, the
poorest of all the beggars, the worst of all the offenders, the very

---

15. 'Psychotherapists or the Clergy?', op. cit., 208-209.

enemy himself – that these are within me, and that I stand in need of the handout of my own kindness – that I myself am the enemy who must be loved – what then?'[16]

In the light of the third way of experiencing the Higher power, described in his letter to Bill Wilson, Jung would probably have agreed that steps four and five of A. A. can bring about real and lasting change. When recovering alcoholics have asked me to accompany them as they made step five, I witnessed inner healing occurring. That step requires people to have a heartfelt desire to take off their usual masks and to be their true, vulnerable selves. As this desire strengthens, it begins to override a deep-seated fear of rejection which echoes back to childhood. As alcoholics begin to lower their defences and to tell the confidant about the darker side of their natures and to sense the understanding and acceptance of the listener, a wonderful reconciliation begins to take place. In the light of this empathic understanding, they begin to understand, accept, and love themselves as they are, and not as they have pretended to be. I'm sure that such acceptance, in the light of another person's love, mediates the healing love of a merciful God. As St James once wrote: 'Confess your sins to one another, and pray for one another that you may be healed' (Jas 5:16). As a result the dividing wall of division between the acceptable and unacceptable self breaks down (cf Eph 2:14), and the recovering alcoholic is strengthened in his or her innermost self by the Spirit (cf Eph 3:16). At this point the person in recovery goes beyond being dry to become truly sober. This is so because the underlying cause of his or her drinking has been dealt with.

Karen Horney on Neurotic Needs

Like many alcoholics, Bill Wilson was prone to depression. It afflicted him a number of times during his life. Not surprisingly, he tried to understand its causes and to overcome it. While it could have physical origins such as bipolar disorder, or a lack of serotonin in his brain, Wilson said in a letter to a fellow sufferer:

---

16. 'Psychotherapists or the Clergy?', op. cit., 207.

'I suppose about half the old-timers have neurotic hangovers of one sort or another. Certainly I can number myself among them.'[17] Step six of A.A. says that recovering addicts should be entirely ready to have God remove all their defects of character. Bill Wilson found that Karen Horney's *Neurosis and Human Growth* was very helpful in this regard. Speaking about its author, Wilson wrote: 'I have the highest admiration for her. That gal's insights have been most helpful to me.'[18]

Horney argued that neurotic attitudes could be traced back of a lack of warmth and affection from parents in childhood, often because they were inhibited by neurotic problems of their own. Horney describes some of the harmful things that parents do either intentionally or unintentionally. She points out that they engage in, 'preference for other children, unjust reproaches, unpredictable changes between overindulgence and scornful rejection, unfulfilled promises, and not least important, an attitude towards the child's needs which goes through all gradations from temporary in-consideration to a consistent interfering with the most legitimate wishes of the child, such as disturbing friendships, ridiculing independent thinking, spoiling its interest in its own pursuits.'[19] Inadequate caring of this kind in childhood alienates young people from their true selves while prompting a deep-seated sense of anxiety and hidden anger toward the powerful but indifferent adults. As a result, neurotic people subsequently spend an inordinate amount of time trying to cope with their anxiety and anger. Typically, they do this by avoiding, attacking, or completely complying with others. These three attitudes could be described as follows.

1. A compliant, self-effacing attitude says implicitly, 'If you love me, you will not hurt me.'
2. An aggressive, expansive attitude says implicitly, 'If I have power, no one can hurt me.'

---

17. *The Soul of Sponsorship*, op. cit. 36.
18. Letter Jan 4th 1956.
19. *The Neurotic Personality of our Time* (New York: Norton, 1937), 80-81.

3. A withdrawn, resigned attitude says implicitly, 'If I with-draw, nothing can hurt me.'[20]

Wilson was particularly impressed by the fact that Horney's book indicated that neurotic people were often motivated by an unhealthy drive for glory and a morbid sense of dependency. The search for glory is a drive that an idealised self-image event-ually grows into, when neurotic conflicts go unaddressed. This compulsive, indiscriminate, insatiable urge to express the ideal-ised self is also accompanied by the need for perfection, neurotic ambition, and the need for vindictive triumph. Like any neurotic drive, it causes intense anxiety when frustrated. One of its re-sults is neurotic pride, the mood felt when one lives up to the 'shoulds' of the idealised self. The elder brother in the parable of the Prodigal Son, epitomises this attitude.

The phrase 'morbid dependency' refers to a neurotic need to feel part of something larger and more powerful than oneself. This need often manifests itself as religious devotion, identific-ation with a group or cause, or morbid dependency in a loving relationship. Love appears as the ticket to paradise, where all woes will end. There will be no more feelings of being lost, guilty, and unworthy; no more responsibility for self; no more struggle with a harsh world for which one feels 'hopelessly un-equipped'.

In 1958 Wilson published an article entitled, 'The New Frontier Emotional Sobriety' in *The Grapevine* magazine. It was quite clear that it had been influenced by Horney's writings. Wilson said: 'I kept asking myself, Why can't the Twelve Steps work to release my depression?' He went on to answer: 'Suddenly, I realised what the matter was. My basic flaw had al-ways been dependence – almost absolute dependence – on peo-ple or circumstances to supply me with prestige, security and the like. Failing to get these things according to my perfectionist dreams and specifications, I had fought for them. And when

---

20. Cf Christopher Monte, *Beneath the Mask: An Introduction to Theories of Personality* (Fort Worth: Harcourt Brace Jovanovich College Publishers, 1991), 590.

defeat came, so did my depression.' In a way Bill Wilson's depression proved to be a blessing in disguise, in the sense that it forced him to acknowledge his inordinate attachments. Whereas psychology had provided the insight, his prayerful spirituality and reliance on God's grace helped him to overcome his neuroses, and hence his depression. He wrote: 'I could not avail myself of God's love until I was able to offer it back to Him by loving others as he would have me. And I couldn't possibly do that so long as I was victimised by false dependencies.'

A.A. Comes to Ireland

Former Secretary of State, Henry Kissinger maintained that A.A. was America's greatest export in the twentieth century. In 1943, it spread to Australia when a group was formed in Sydney. Fr Tom Dunlea, an Irish priest who was connected with A.A. in Sydney, visited Ireland in 1946. While in Dublin, he was interviewed by the *Evening Mail*. He spoke at some length about the success of the Sydney group of A.A. His description of how the fellowship operated was not strictly accurate but, that said, he was the first person to introduce A.A. to the general public in Ireland. At about the same time Conor F., an Irish American, visited Ireland from Philadelphia. He had been sober for three years and was determined to form an A.A. group in Dublin before he returned to the US. He met a non-alcoholic lady called Eva Jennings who arranged for him to meet a Dr Moore from St Patrick's Hospital who, in turn, put him in touch with Richard, a chronic alcoholic. Their coming together in November 1946 was the first A.A. meeting held in Ireland.[21] It may also have been the first A.A. meeting in Europe.[22] The first A.A. group meetings in Ireland took place, weekly, in a room called 'The Country Shop' on St Stephen's Green. Nowadays there are about 780 A.A. groups in the country with an estimated membership of between 15 and 20,000.

21. Apparently, Richard never took another drink after that providential get-together.
22. 'Focus on Addiction: The Spirituality of A.A.', *Intercom* (June 2005), 34.

Conclusion

It is arguable that as materialism and individualism have increased in our secularised, Western culture, lack of a joyful sense of ultimate belonging is leading to increased levels of addiction as many psychologists had predicted. The word addiction comes from Latin, and means: 'to hand over into the care of someone else'. As a result, the addicted person is no longer under his or her own control. Gerald May says that an addiction is 'any compulsive, habitual behaviour that limits the freedom of human desire. It is caused by attachment, or nailing of desire to specific objects.'[23] In his wise book, *Addiction and Grace*, May says, that in contemporary society the question is not *whether* people have an addiction, but rather, what addictions, out of a list of 200 or more, *have they really got*. Addictions are what used to be called inordinate attachments, activities that nail down transcendental desires for meaning and God, to created things. In other words they are forms of idolatry and contrary to the first commandment.

In a section on addiction in *Dark Night of the Soul: A Psychiatrist Explores the Connection Between Darkness and Growth*, Gerald May points out that, in order to escape addiction, people in 12 step programmes can end up addicted to recovery. That is why some observers say of people in recovery that they replace addiction to alcohol with addiction to A.A. Instead of being the supreme end of human devotion, worthy of appreciation and gratitude, the person in recovery sees God as a means to his or her sobriety. Hopefully, says May, people on the road to recovery would begin to notice that what began as a desperate need for God can change into a loving desire for God. Instead of being a means to an end, God can become the supreme end of one's life. 'It is as if God were saying, Of course I want to be your saving Higher Power, but I also want to be so much more to you. I want to be your deepest love.'[24]

Together, Alcoholics Anonymous and modern psychologists

23. (San Francisco: Harper & Row, 1988),
24. (San Francisco: Harper, 2004), 162.

have united to say something significant to contemporary society about the relationship between therapy and spirituality. Through their complementarity they avoid spiritualising psychology on the one hand, or psychologising spirituality on the other. Together they bear united witness to the fact that people will not be freed from addiction, and by extension, from any form of neurosis, until they have a genuine experience of the Higher Power, i.e. God consciousness. Toward the end of *The Big Book,* we read these salutary words: 'Most emphatically we wish to say that any alcoholic capable of honestly facing his problems in the light of our experience can recover, provided he does not close his mind to spiritual concepts. He can only be defeated by an attitude of intolerance or belligerent denial.'[25]

---

25. Op. cit., 568.

CHAPTER FIVE

ESP and Inspired Words of Knowledge

I'm fascinated by mechanical gadgets such as radio controlled watches, hand held computers, MP3 players and the like. My current favourite is a satellite navigation system, known as a GPS (i.e. global positioning system). This computerised gismo is used by people who travel by road. They enter their departure point and destination into the GPS. It works out the best way of getting there with the aid of geostationary satellites orbiting 27,000 miles above the earth. It has a twofold ability to offer guidance. Firstly, an arrow offers precise visual directions on a coloured map which is displayed on a screen. Secondly, a woman's voice gives specific instructions. If perchance the driver makes a mistake, the mellifluous voice graciously suggests an alternative way of getting to the destination, without a hint of criticism. Since purchasing a GPS I have rarely consulted a map for directions or got lost. It has struck me on a number of occasions that the Holy Spirit is a bit like a spiritual GPS. It can give those who are tuned into its inspirations the guidance needed for the journey to God. If perchance we make a mistake or ignore its promptings, the Spirit doesn't condemn us. Rather it suggests an alternative way of reaching our destination. Is it any surprise, therefore, that St Paul says, 'Be guided by the Spirit' (Gal 5:18)?

Christians receive guidance in a number of ways, e.g. through the commandments, the beatitudes and the ethical teachings of the scriptures, and through the exercise of legitimate religious authority in the church. However, in everyday life we have often to discern with the Spirit's help what it is we are supposed to do. As George Montague has written: 'When confronted by any moral decision, great or small, the Christian's first question should be, Where does the Spirit lead me in this?'[1] It is not my intention to explain here how the Spirit guides us in the choices of everyday life. I have done so elsewhere.[2] In this chapter I want to focus on an unusual form of guidance, called the word of knowledge. It is mostly associated with Pentecostal and Charismatic Christians, notably Kathryn Kuhlman, Oral Roberts, Ralph di Orio, Emilien Tardif and Briege Mc Kenna. John Wimber described the gift in these words: 'A word of knowledge is God revealing facts about a situation concerning which a person had no previous knowledge. An example of this is God giving someone exact details of a person's life, to reveal sin, warn and provide safety, reveal thoughts, provide healing or provide instructions.'[3] Because many readers will be unfamiliar with this unusual phenomenon, we will begin by examining it from a scriptural, theological and experiential point of view. Then we will go on to see what light psychology and parapsychology can throw upon it.

The Word of Knowledge in the Bible

Whenever religious people claim to receive guidance from God there are always skeptics who question whether it is genuine. There are two kinds of objection that they commonly raise. Firstly, there are those who, because of their secularised world view, have difficulty in believing that God can reveal anything to us.[4] One is reminded in this context of the words of St Paul: 'The man without the Spirit does not accept the things that come from the Spirit of God, for they are foolishness to him' (1 Cor 2:14). Secondly, when people claim to have been guided by God to do some questionable deed, such as President George Bush maintaining that God inspired him to invade Iraq, they bring the notion of divine guidance into disrepute. There is a Latin saying

---

1. *The Holy Spirit: Growth of a Biblical Tradition* (New York: Paulist Press, 1976), 200.
2. 'Seeking God's Will in Prayer', *Prayer in Practice: A Biblical Approach* (Dublin: Columba, 2000), 91-113.
3. *Power Healing,* (London: Hodder & Stoughton, 1986), 204.
4. Cf Part I of Morton Kelsey, *Encounter With God: A Theology of Christian Experience* (London: Hodder & Stoughton, 1974).

abusus non tollit usum, which is relevant here. Translated into English it states, 'the abuse of anything does not invalidate its correct use.' Prayerful people of goodwill can and do receive guidance from God. The Old and New Testaments endorse this point of view. Let's look at some indicative texts.

A favourite Old Testament text speaks about revelation from God. In Jer 33:3-4 we read: 'Call to me and I will answer you and tell you great and unsearchable things you do not know.' Similar promises are made in the New Testament. Here are just two examples. Jesus promised: 'When he, the Spirit of truth comes, he will guide you into all truth. He will not speak on his own; he will speak only what he hears, and he will tell you what is yet to come' (Jn 16:13). The apostle John explained: 'As for you, the anointing you received from him remains in you, and you do not need anyone to teach you. But his anointing teaches you about all things' (1 Jn 2:27). Because he believed in this kind of divine inspiration St Paul testified that: 'We have not stopped praying for you and asking God to fill you with the knowledge of his will through all spiritual wisdom and understanding' (Col 1:9).

St Paul says that one of the unusual ways of receiving divine guidance is through the word of knowledge. The most important New Testament reference to this mysterious gift is to be found in 1 Cor 12:8 where St Paul says: 'To one there is given through the Spirit ... a message of knowledge by means of the ... Spirit.' Most of the well known scholars who have commented on 1 Cor 12:8, such as Carson, Kristemaker and Bittlinger,[5] say that the word of knowledge refers to an inspired ability to preach and teach the good news. However, speaking of the charism of knowledge, Gordon Fee, an eminent Pentecostal scholar, says in *God's Empowering Presence* that while the 'utterance of knowledge' can take the form of inspired teaching, it can

5. D. A. Carson, *Showing the Spirit: A Theological Exposition of 1 Corinthians 12-14* (Carlisle: Paternoster Press, 1987), 38; Simon Kistemaker, *1 Corinthians* (Grand Rapids: Baker, 1994), 421; Arnold Bittlinger, *Gifts and Graces: A Commentary on 1 Corinthians 12-14* (London: Hodder & Stoughton, 1967), 30-31.

also refer to 'a supernatural endowment of knowledge, factual information that could not otherwise have been known without the Spirit's aid, such as frequently occurs in the prophetic tradition.'[6] Catholic scripture scholar George Montague concurs when he writes: 'In the history of the Christian interpretation of this gift two different meanings have been attached to it: one concerns an inspired knowledge of a fact, the other an inspired insight into the Christian mystery granted especially for the purpose of teaching.'[7] I was interested to see that Anglican bishop, David Pytches, endorses Fee's and Montague's interpretation. He states that the word of knowledge is a: 'supernatural revelation of facts about a person or situation, which is not learned through the efforts of the natural mind, but is a fragment of knowledge freely given by God, disclosing the truth which the Spirit wishes to be made known concerning a particular person or situation.'[8] In this chapter we will concentrate on this second interpretation.

There is one verse in St Paul's writings that I find particularly helpful when it comes to understanding the prophetic word of knowledge. In 1 Cor 2:10-11 he writes: 'The Spirit searches all things, even the deep things of God.' Paul seems to be suggesting that the Spirit has an intimate knowledge both of all created things and the mystery of God. The word 'intimate' in English is derived from Latin and could loosely be translated as 'to publish, to make known that which is innermost.' There is an implication that the Spirit of God is familiar with the hidden essence of everything that exists. Like an X-ray it penetrates in a loving, affirming way to the 'isness' of everything. In this context one is reminded of a verse in Wis 1:7 which says: 'For the spirit of the Lord fills the world, and that which holds everything together, knows every word said.' If that is true of creation in general, it is particularly true of human beings. Not only is the Holy Spirit ac-

---

6. (Peabody, Mass: Hendrickson, 1995), 167.
7. *The Holy Spirit*, op. cit., 151.
8. *Come Holy Spirit: Learning to Minister in Power* (London: Hodder & Stoughton, 1985), 99.

quainted with the inner reality of every cell in the body, more importantly, it is *au fait* with every nuance of human subjectivity, with all of its thoughts, memories and desires. God's Spirit knows us better than we know ourselves; nothing is hidden from its penetrating but benevolent gaze. At the same time the Spirit also has an intimate knowledge of the infinite depths of God. We could say, in a rather anthropomorphic way, that the Spirit is familiar with the thoughts, memories and desires of God. Historically, they were manifested in the humanity of Christ, especially through his life, death and resurrection. Paul then goes on to say that God's Holy Spirit has been poured into the hearts of believers. In principle, therefore, graced individuals can, like Christ, know others, their bodies, minds and spirits, as God knows them, by means of the Spirit's activity. Sometimes they will also have a sense of what God wants for the people they know in this intimate spiritual way. It is quite possible that these supernatural abilities build upon right brained capacities such as intuition and psychic sensitivities of an extra-sensory kind. This possibility will be examined below.

Old and New Testament Examples
There are many instances of the word of knowledge in the Old Testament. We will advert to just three of many possible examples. The prophet Nathan knew about David's sin of adultery with Bathsheba, and he uses the parable about the poor man and the lamb before confronting him by saying, 'You are that man' (2 Sam 12:1-12). Daniel had an inspired sense that Susanna was innocent of the accusations made by the two randy old men and devised a test which exposed their guilt and the woman's innocence (Dan 13:44-49). When Saul was chosen as king, he hid himself. We are told, however, that the people 'inquired further of the Lord, "Has the man come here yet?" And the Lord said, (presumably through someone in the gathering uttering a prophetic word of knowledge) "Yes, he has hidden himself among the baggage". (1 Sam 10:22).

In the New Testament we are told that Jesus seemed to be

able to read people's hearts and to predict future events. For instance, he appeared to know all about Nathaniel although he had never met him before (Jn 1:48), and he was able to tell the Samaritan woman at the well that she hadn't one husband, but five (Jn 4:18). When asked to pay the tax, Jesus knew about the four drachma coin in the fish's mouth, which Peter would later retrieve (Mt 17:27). On another occasion, Jesus told the disciples that they would find a donkey in a certain place (Mk 11:2) and that they would meet with a man carrying a pitcher of water (Mk 14:13). During his scourging at the pillar the Roman soldiers taunted the blindfolded Jesus, by saying: 'Prophesy, who hit you?' This indicated that Jesus was known to have an ability to speak words of knowledge. Par 521 of the *Catechism of the Catholic Church* spells out the implications for contemporary Christians when it says that: 'Christ enables us to live in him, all that he himself lived and he lives it in us.' That means, if God so wills it, a Christian can be enabled by the Spirit to exercise the gift of the prophetic word of knowledge.

In the New Testament church some of the believers were granted the word of knowledge. For example, we are told that on one occasion the prophet Agabus: 'stood up and through the Spirit predicted that a severe famine would spread over the entire Roman world. This happened during the reign of Claudius' (Acts 11:28). Ananias and Saul met as a result of words of knowledge: 'The Lord told him, "Go to the house of Judas on Straight Street and ask for a man from Tarsus named Saul, for he is praying. In a vision he has seen a man named Ananias come and place his hands on him to restore his sight"' (Acts 9:11-12). St Peter met with Cornelius in much the same way when he and the centurion received words of knowledge (Acts 10:17-23).

In the writings of St Paul it is fairly clear that the word of knowledge has the power to evoke the charism of faith which is mentioned in 1 Cor 12:9; 13:2. Speaking about this unusual gift, George Montague explains: 'The gift of faith in 1 Cor 12:9 does not refer to the faith that is necessary for salvation (Mk 16:16; Heb 11:6), but rather to a special intensity of faith for a specific need.'[9] David Pytches accurately describes the charism of faith as, 'a supernatural surge of confidence from the Spirit of God which arises within a person faced with a specific situation of need whereby that person receives a trans-rational certainty and assurance that God is about to act through a word or action.'[10] It is significant that there is only one place in the New Testament where we are told how faith grows. Paul says in Rom 10:17-18, 'faith comes from hearing the message (*rehema*), and the message is heard through the word of Christ.' It is worth noting that *rehema*, the Greek word for message, refers to the revelatory word that is spoken in the here-and-now, to a particular person or group. It is this living word that evokes the mustard seed of certainty in the heart, about what God *is* doing in the present, rather than what God *might* do in the future.

The word of knowledge can be granted in the form of an inspiring verse/s from scripture, a prophetic intuition, an interior picture, or intellectual understanding, in such a way that the person has no lingering doubts about the promises of God. Once s/he knows God's existential will, they can pray either a prayer of intercession (Mk 11:24) or command (Mk 11:23) with complete assurance. As 1 Jn 5:14 says, 'And this is the confidence we have in God, that if we ask for anything according to his will, he hears us. And if we know that he hears us in whatever we ask, we know that we have obtained the requests made of him.' In other words it is not a matter of praying with future hope, if what we ask for is in accordance with God's will. Rather, it is a matter of praying with present conviction because we already know that what we ask for is God's will. The charism of expectant faith is mainly expressed by means of the charisms of power listed in 1 Cor 12:10 such as healing/exorcism and miracle working.

---

9. *The Holy Spirit*, op cit., 152
10. *Come Holy Spirit*, op. cit., 109

Contemporary Experience

Many of us have heard of charismatic people like John Vianney and Padre Pio of Pietrelcina who were blessed with 'words of knowledge' of different kinds, such as an ability to foretell future events and to read people's hearts. For example, a woman whose husband had committed suicide by drowning went to see the Curé of Ars. She was tormented by the fear that he might be damned and wondered if the saintly priest could offer her any cause for hope. Before she had time to share her worry John Vianney said, 'Do not worry. Between the bridge and the water your husband repented, and made an act of contrition. Pray for him.'[11] Padre Pio had similar gifts. We are told that on one occasion Padre Dionisio told his confrère that he intended to go to Venice to pursue further studies. 'Studies! Studies!' Pio cried, 'Think of death!' Bewildered and offended, Padre Dionisio went away, while Padre Pio shrugged his shoulders and said to a colleague, 'There is nothing I can do.' Twenty days later Padre Dionisio dropped dead.[12]

In the twentieth century a number of well known charismatics exercised similar gifts. I suppose the person who was best known for this activity was the late Kathryn Kuhlman. She exercised a healing ministry for many years in the USA. What made her unusual was the fact that she didn't pray for healing with the laying on of hands. Instead she would talk and pray until she received an anointing of the Holy Spirit. Then, inspired by words of knowledge, she would say who was being healed of what ailment in specific areas of the auditorium. The following words are taken from a transcript of one of her miracle services. 'There is a heart condition disappearing. Wonderful Jesus, I give you praise and glory ... There is a case of sugar diabetes ... the sugar is draining from your body ... an ear has been opened completely. Someone hears me perfectly. In the balcony. Check

---

11. Henri Gehon, 'The Secret of the Curé of Ars', *Secrets of the Saints*, (London: Sheed & Ward, 1973), 65.
12. Cf Bernard Ruffin, *Padre Pio: The True Story* (Huntington: Our Sunday Visitor, 1982), 267.

on that someone. Up there in the top left balcony is a man with a hearing aid. Check that ear, sir. Hold your good ear closed tight; you hear me perfectly.' Speaking about her exercise of this remarkable gift Kathryn said: 'My mind is so surrendered to the Spirit that I know the exact body being healed; the sickness, the affliction, and in some instances the very sin in their lives. And yet I do not pretend to tell you why or how.'[13]

The late John Wimber, founder of the Vineyard Fellowship in Anaheim, California, was blessed with the same gift. In his book *Power Evangelism: Signs and Wonders Today*, he recounted a very interesting experience. He was flying from Chicago to New York. He said that during the flight he noticed a business man in a nearby seat. Then in his mind's eye he could see the word adultery written across his face. By now the man had become aware of the fact that Wimber was staring at him. 'What do you want?' he snapped. Wimber says that, as he spoke, a woman's name came into his mind. So he leaned across and asked if the name meant anything to him. The man's face drained of colour. 'We have to talk,' he stammered. 'Who told you that name?' 'God told me,' retorted Wimber. 'God told you!' 'Yes, he told me to tell you … that unless you turn from this adulterous relationship, he is going to take your life.' In a choking voice the man asked, 'What should I do?' Wimber urged him to repent and to commit himself to Christ. With that, the man burst into tears and cried out, 'O God, I am sorry' … and he launched into the most heart rending repentance Wimber had ever witnessed. The whole incident raises the question, how did John Wimber know those things about a stranger? Was it pure chance, a natural thing like clairvoyance, the Holy Spirit, or a combination of all three?

Over the years I have found that that 'words of knowledge', in whatever way they are received, can be invaluable in different ministry situations. Firstly, in the sacrament of reconciliation some priests will occasionally know a penitent's secret sins. This

---

13. Kathryn Kuhlman, *I Believe in Miracles* (London: Lakeland, 1974), 199.

knowledge enables them to help him or her to make a good confession. I had that experience once with a murderer who really
repented. Secondly, the Lord can guide intercessory prayer by
means of a 'word of knowledge.' At a prayer meeting in
Northern Ireland, for example, I heard a woman praying about a
very specific trouble spot in Belfast. The next day we found out
from the newspaper that, at the very time she was praying, a car
bomb had failed to go off in the exact location she had been concerned about. Thirdly, those who pray for inner healing are
sometimes led by a 'word of knowledge' to focus on a repressed
memory. A man who was suffering from claustrophobia went to
a priest I know. After a few minutes of prayer the priest said,
'You were nearly drowned when you were three.' Immediately,
the man recalled such a forgotten incident. Following a brief
prayer for healing of memories, his phobia disappeared completely. Fourthly, as the ministry of Kathryn Kuhlman and others
have demonstrated, words of knowledge are sometimes granted
to those praying for physical cures, particularly at healing services.

Not only do the four kinds of 'words of knowledge' guide
the supplications and ministry of pray-ers, as was noted above,
they also evoke the charism of expectant, unhesitating faith. As
Jesus said: 'I tell you the truth, if anyone says to this mountain,
"Go, throw yourself into the sea," and does not doubt in his
heart but believes that what he says will happen, it will be done
for him. Therefore I tell you, whatever you ask for in prayer, believe that you have received it, and it will be yours' (Mk 11:23-24).
Time and time again, I have seen how the word of knowledge can
evoke unhesitating faith and empower effective ministry.

Catholic Theology's Perspective
Catholic theology has long maintained that besides public revelation, which was completed with the death of the last apostle,
there is always the possibility of private revelation. It takes the
form of prophetic inspirations that are granted to particular individuals, such as the messages given by Our Lady to Catherine

Labouré in the Rue de Bac in Paris or to Faustina Kowalska in Vilnius. As such they are classified as mystical phenomena, of a revelatory kind, which are characteristic of the illuminative stage of the Christian life. Well known Catholic writers such as Baron Von Hugel,[14] R. P. Poulain,[15] Jordan Aumann[16] and Harvey Egan[17] have written about this kind of private revelation.

St Thomas Aquinas wrote quite extensively on the charisms in 1 Cor 12:8-10. His reflections can be found in three places, his biblical commentary on the First Letter to the Corinthians,[18] in a section on the gratuitous graces in his *Summa Theologica*,[19] and in a section on gratuitous graces in the *Summa Contra Gentiles*.[20] Like a number of scripture scholars, St Thomas relates the gift of knowledge to the gift of prophecy. 'Some charisms,' he says 'freely given relate to knowledge ... Those relating to knowledge can be summed up in the word prophecy ... Prophecy consists first and foremost in knowing certain far-off things outside the normal knowledge of men ... Prophetic knowledge relies on God's light in which all things are visible, human and divine, bodily and spiritual, so that anything whatever can be the subject of prophetic revelation. But secondarily it involves speech, since a prophet proclaims to others what God has taught him in order to build them up. And finally prophets sometimes work miracles to confirm their prophecies.'[21]

---

14. *The Mystical Element in Religion as Studied in St Catherine of Genoa and her Friends* (1909)

15. 'Revelations and Visions', *The Graces of Interior Prayer: A Treatise on Mystical Theology* (London: Keegan Paul, 1910), 299-399.

16. 'Revelations', *Spiritual Theology* (London: Sheed & Ward, 1982), 428-431.

17. 'Prophecy', *Christian Mysticism: The Future of a Tradition* (New York: Pueblo, 1984), 321-322.

18. Cf Thomas Aquinas, *The Gifts of the Spirit: Selected Spiritual Writings*, ed. Benedict Ashley, (New York: New City Press, 1995), 33.

19. 'Charisms', *Summa Theologiae: A Concise Translation*, ed. Timothy Mc Dermott, (London: Methuen, 1989), 338-339; 444-451.

20. Book 3, chap 155.

21. *Summa Theologiae: A Concise Translation*, op. cit., 444-445.

Thomas also describes some ways in which enlightenment can be experienced: 'Now, accompanying this light that we have mentioned (i.e. of faith) which illumines the mind from within, there are at times in divine revelation other external or internal aids to knowledge; for instance, a spoken message, or something heard by the external senses (presumably hearing) which is produced by divine power, or something perceived internally is seen in bodily visions, or that are internally pictured in the imagination. From these presentations, by the light internally impressed on the mind, man receives a knowledge of divine things.'[22] Although it is true that Thomas may be thinking here about the way in which the gift of knowledge enables a person to appreciate the mystery of God in Christ, his reflections can be extended in such a way as to embrace the prophetic word of knowledge.

In the years between 1734-38 Cardinal Prospero Lambertini, later to be Benedict XIV, wrote a four volume work entitled, *De Beatificatione Servorum Dei et De Canonizatione Beatorum*, (Of the Beatification of the Servants of God and the Canonisation of the Blessed). As a man of immense erudition, Cardinal Lambertini was well qualified to write his *magnum opus*. It assessed the criteria to be used in making a judgement as to whether a person was saintly or not. One of the aspects he considered was a spectrum of charismatic activities from speaking in tongues to miracle working. Relying on St Thomas Aquinas, he said that these charisms were gratuitous graces rather than sanctifying ones. In other words, they were given to sanctify others rather than the people who exercised them. As such, they were not necessarily signs of holiness.

In the course of his examination of different charismatic phenomena, Lambertini spent some time evaluating the gift of prophecy. He defined it as 'one whereby a man may know and make known matters of which he could not become aware by any normal means: future, past or distant or hidden present

---

22. *Summa Contra Gentiles*, book 3, par 155.

things, or the secrets of hearts, or inward thoughts.'[23] He says
that there is a natural version of this gift, what he refers to variously as 'the prophetic instinct,' 'natural prophecy' and a 'natural
gift of divination.' From what he says, it looks as if he included
the preternatural powers of telepathy, clairvoyance and precognition in this category.

He went on to describe three ways in which people were
granted the prophetic word of knowledge. His teaching reflects
that of St Thomas. Firstly, it could be experienced by means of
hallucinations that correspond to or represent true events or
persons, in which something is perceived, 'as if through the bodily senses.' Examples of this would be 'crisis apparitions' in
which the figure of a person dying or in danger in some other
distant place is 'seen' by someone who loves that person.
Secondly, such knowledge can come 'by means of an inward
sense', i.e. an inward image or picture that wells up in the mind.
The third form of revelation is through an imageless intellectual
awareness. He says that these prophetic words can anticipate
future events before they occur either because they are implicit
in current events or because they are directly revealed by God.
Renee Haynes makes the interesting suggestion that in Jungian
terms the first form of prophecy might be a characteristic of
sensing types, the second of feeling types, and the third of intuitive types.[24] It would appear that, in his classic work on beatification and canonisation, Cardinal Lambertini, thought that
paranormal powers, however they are explained, can be involved in graced words of knowledge. Apparently, he was fond
of quoting from St Thomas Aquinas, 'not all the secondary causes
in the working of created nature' are yet known.[25]

Psychological Aspects of the Gift
Having described the word of knowledge in a spiritual way, we

---

23. Quoted by Renee Haynes, 'The Holy and the Paranormal',
Philosopher King: The Humanist Pope Benedict XIV (London: Weidenfeld
and Nicolson, 1970), 100.
24. *Philosopher King*, op. cit., 101.
25. *Philosopher King*, op. cit., 31.

need to move on to ask, what would psychology have to say about the claims of Pentecostals and Charismatics who claim to have received such inspired intimations.

a) Empathic Intuition

One could ask whether the word of knowledge was made possible by a combination of empathy and intuition. Empathy as we know, is the ability to enter and understand the world of another person. Empathy is often associated with intuition as a kind of knowledge gained through emotional identification. It is a sympathy whereby a person is carried into the interior of a person so as to coincide with what is unique and inexpressible in him or her. At times it seems to be independent of sensory experience or reasoning. Philosopher Jacques Maritain has said that intuition 'is not rational knowledge, knowledge through the conceptual, logical, and discursive exercise of reason. But it is really and genuinely knowledge, though obscure and perhaps incapable of giving an account of itself.'[26] It could be argued that empathy and intuition might be involved in a word of knowledge, especially in the context of one-to-one relationships where the person is aware of body-language and feelings. But it seems highly unlikely that it is involved when healers get words of knowledge at large services, because there is no sensory or empathic contact with the particular individuals present.

b) Extra Sensory Perception

In the mid eighties a large Charismatic conference was held in Sheffield City Hall. John Wimber and his team ministered to the 2,800 participants. Dr David Lewis from the Alister Hardy Research Centre in Oxford attended. Afterwards he wrote a report on what he witnessed, entitled 'Signs and wonders at Sheffield, a social anthropologist's analysis of words of knowledge, manifestations of the Spirit and the effectiveness of divine

---

26. 'Creative Intuition and Poetic Knowledge', *A Maritain Reader* (New York: Image, 1966), 332.

healing.'[27] Because this chapter is concentrating on words of knowledge we will focus on what Lewis had to say about this phenomenon.

Apparently, the gift was much in evidence at healing workshops during the conference. Lewis considered whether words of knowledge about ailments were explainable on the basis of statistical probability. For example, if someone said, 'I think there is someone here with lower back pain', it is likely that half the people in the audience would identify with the word. But if the word of knowledge was more specific, then the odds of it being due to a lucky guess would begin to increase. The person uttering the word might say, 'There is a man over here, on the left hand side of the audience, about two thirds of the way down, who has a badly damaged disk in his lower back ever since he was involved in a car accident eight years ago.' The fact that he said it was a man would rule out all the women, the fact that he specified where the man was in the audience would rule out even more people. But when he specified the problem was due to a damaged disk in the lower part of the spine, the car accident and the time it occurred, the odds against him guessing the injury by chance would be very high indeed. And if this was done, time and time again as it was at Sheffield, Lewis concluded that the words of knowledge he heard were virtually impossible to explain in terms of chance.

Lewis then went on to ask whether the words of knowledge could be explained in another way. He wrote: 'An obvious hypothesis is that words of knowledge come from some sort of extra-sensory perception (ESP) such as telepathy or clairvoyance.'[28] Telepathy, refers to direct mind-to-mind communication between individuals in which all other means of communication have been excluded. Clairvoyance is the experience of perceiving objects, events, or people too far away to see using the five senses. Although Lewis doesn't mention precognition it

27. Appendix D, *Power Healing*, op. cit., 252-273.
28. *Memories, Dreams, Reflections*, op. cit., 335-336.

could also have been involved in the words of knowledge. It is an ability to have direct knowledge of future events. Lewis admits that these para-psychological abilities are controversial. As was mentioned in a previous chapter, ESP, if it exists, is natural. Catholic theology is not necessarily against it. Because Catholics believe that grace builds on nature, they would not be too surprised if ESP was involved in prophetic words of knowledge.

A Quantum Physicist on ESP

A number of years ago I read an article about David Bohm who was a protégé of Einstein and the author of a standard work on quantum physics. What made Bohm different from many other scientists was the fact that, from childhood, he had a mystical sense, one that was experientially aware of the oneness of the created world. In adult life, this unitary sense influenced the way in which he approached physics. He wrote eloquently about the world as if it were a giant hologram in which the whole is always present in each of its parts, no matter how small they might be.[29] Holograms are created by an advanced form of laser photography that allows an image to be recorded in three dimensions. The objects photographed can be reproduced as 3D images of light. This is made possible by lasers that read the holographic image from a metal photographic plate. No matter how often the plate is divided, e.g. into half its size, a quarter of its size etc., the lasers can still reproduce the whole image, albeit at a proportionately lower degree of clarity. The implication is that, each part of the photographic plate contains the whole image. Bohm believes that the universe has the characteristics of a giant hologram. Commenting on Bohm's views, renowned brain scientist Karl Pribram has said, 'if you look at the universe with a holographic system, you arrive at a different view, a different reality. And that other reality can explain things that have hitherto remained inexplicable scientifically: paranormal phen-

---

29. Cf Renee Weber, 'The Enfolding-Unfolding Universe: A Conversation with David Bohm', *The Holographic Paradigm and Other Paradoxes*, ed. Ken Wilber (Bolder, Colorado: Shambhala, 1982), 44-104.

omena, synchronicities, and the apparently meaningful coincidence of events.'[30]

Using this holographic image, Bohm suggested that reality has an implicate dimension that involves a process of movement, continuous unfolding and enfolding from a seamless whole which embrace the realms of matter, life and consciousness. His theory is a complex one. We will not go into it here. Suffice it to say that when asked in an interview to explain the concept of enfoldment, Bohm responded: 'Everybody has seen an image of enfoldment: You fold up a sheet of paper, turn it into a small packet, make cuts in it, and then unfold it into a pattern. The parts that were close in the cuts unfold to be far away. This is like what happens in a hologram. Enfoldment is really very common in our experience. All the light in this room comes in so that the entire room is in effect folded into each part. If your eye looks, the light will be then unfolded by your eye and brain. As you look through a telescope or a camera, the whole universe of space and time is enfolded into each part, and that is unfolded to the eye. With an old-fashioned television set that's not adjusted properly, the image enfolds into the screen and then can be unfolded by adjustment.'[31] One is reminded in this connection of a verse of visionary poet, William Blake: 'To see a world in a grain of sand, and a heaven in a wild flower, hold infinity in the palm of your hand, and eternity in an hour.'[32] Bohm argued that once scientists moved from a materialistic to a more holistic view of reality, they would be able to explain para-psychological phenomena such as telepathy, clairvoyance and precognition.

A Significant Experiment
In 1982 a scientist called Alain Aspect carried out an experiment, known as EPR because it had been proposed by Einstein, Podolsky and Rosen in 1935. David Bohm and one of his sup-

---

30. Interview in *Psychology Today*, quoted by Michael Talbot, *The Holographic Universe* (New York: Harper/Collins, 1991), 11.
31. This interview with David Bohm, conducted by F. David Peat and John Briggs, appeared in *Omni*, (January 1987).
32. *Auguries of Innocence*.

porters, John Bell of CERN, i.e. the European organisation for research into nuclear physics, supported this work. In 1964, John
Bell, an Irishman, developed a mathematical proof that supported
a non-physical dimension of the universe. Bell's Theorem stated
that any model explaining the universe entirely as local or as
physical reality is incomplete for it does not include the non-
local part. He also stated that there is an interconnectedness to
everything in the universe. The EPR experiments demonstrated
that if two quantum systems interact and then move apart, their
behaviour is correlated in a way that cannot be explained in
terms of signals travelling between them at, or slower than, the
speed of light. This phenomenon is known as non-locality, and
is open to two main interpretations: either it involves unmediated,
instantaneous action at a distance, or it involves faster-than-light
signalling. In 1983 the *Sunday Times* reported that experimental
verification of the hypothesis had taken place because two sub-
atomic particles behaved harmoniously as if it 'knew' what the
other particle was doing.[33] The implications of this discovery
were momentous. Victor Mansfield has written in his book
Synchronicity, Science, and Soul-Making: 'Nonlocality or non-sep-
arability is asking us to revise completely our ideas about objects, to remove a pervasive projection we have upon nature. We
can no longer consider objects as independently existing entities
that can be localised in well-defined regions of space-time. They
are interconnected in ways not even conceivable using ideas
from classical physics, which is largely a refinement and extrap-
olation from our normal macroscopic sense of functioning.'[34]

Commenting on these findings, David Bohm said: 'It may
seem that everything in the universe is in a kind of total rapport,
so that whatever happens is related to everything else; or it may
mean that there is some kind of information that can travel faster
than the speed of light; or it may mean that our concepts of space
and time have to be modified in some way which we don't know
or understand. Yet, whichever interpretation you choose, the ex-

33. Science section, Feb 20th
34. (Chicago: Open Court, 1995), 122.

periment establishes once and for all that physics as we know it is unfinished.'[35] I was interested to see that one writer maintains that Bohm thought that telepathy and clairvoyance may be a form of psychokinesis. Just as psychokinesis is a fragment of meaning conveyed from a mind to a material object, ESP could be seen as a resonance of meaning conveyed from one mind to another. He says: 'When a harmony or resonance of meanings is established, the action works both ways, so that the meanings of the distant system could act in the viewer to produce a kind of inverse psychokinesis that would, in effect, transmit an image of that system to him.'[36]

The notion of nonlocality has been invoked as a possible explanation for telepathy and clairvoyance, though Bohm believed that they might involve a deeper level of nonlocality, or what he called 'super-nonlocality'. It would mean that information could be 'received' at a distance at exactly the same moment as it was generated, without undergoing any form of transmission. An alternative explanation is that information – which is basically a pattern of energy – always takes time to travel from its source to another location, that information is stored at some paraphysical level, and that we can access this information, or exchange information with other minds, if the necessary conditions of 'sympathetic resonance' exist. Carl Jung anticipated these findings in his autobiography *Memories, Dreams, Reflections*. He wrote, 'There are indications that at least part of the psyche is not subject to the laws of space and time. Scientific proof has been provided by the well known J. B. experiments.[37] Along with numerous cases of spontaneous foreknowledge, non-spatial perceptions and so on ... these experiments prove that the psyche at times functions outside of the spatio-temporal law of causality.'[38] Bohm's theory seems to say that not only has each person an

35. Quoted by Andrew Samuels, *Jung and the Post-Jungians* (London: Routledge & Keegan Paul, 1986), 30.
36. Quoted by Michael Talbot, *The Holographic Universe* (New York: Harper Perennial, 1992), 145-146.
37. J. B. Rhine, a pioneer in parapsychological research.
38. (London: Fontana, 1972), 335.

unconscious mind, in some strange way it also participates in the collective unconscious of the universe. The notion of unconsciousness here could be understood, perhaps, in terms of Teilhard de Chardin's description of the inwardness of things being proportionate to their material complexity, a sort of incipient or inchoate form of consciousness.[39]

More Evidence is Needed

Many readers may have found the last few paragraphs hard to understand. But what they do establish is that a major thinker from the scientific community has proposed a theory that would go some way to explaining the phenomenon of ESP. However, it has to be said that Bohm's ideas remain unproven. He was working on some mathematical model before he died in 1994, one that would have been amenable to experimental testing. As far as I know, either he didn't have enough time to complete his calculations or found that there were intangible elements in his theory which were difficult, if not impossible, to prove in an empirical way. That said, he has provided us with a tentative scientific way of understanding the telepathic, clairvoyant or precognitive powers that may be involved in the charismatic exercise of the prophetic word of knowledge.

When Dr Lewis attended the Wimber conference in Sheffield he felt that it was unlikely that telepathy was involved in words of knowledge. He argued that telepathy usually works between people who know one another well, e.g. twins, members of a family, or close friends. People attending a conference were not close in this sense. He also thought that it was unlikely that telepathy would account for the fact that a person uttering a word of knowledge might say, for instance, that there were eleven people in the audience suffering from a particular complaint such as arthritis of the left hip. He couldn't see how telepathy could be so specific. He says that if people were trans-

---

39. Cf. Teilhard de Chardin, 'Turmoil or Genesis?', *Science and Religion: New Perspectives on the Dialogue,* ed. Ian Barbour, (London: SCM, 1968), 221.

mitting information like radios, it was unlikely that a gifted person could receive many simultaneous transmissions and be able to say exactly what the number was. He implies therefore, that the gift of the word of knowledge is more supernatural than natural.

From, my own experience of witnessing and exercising the word of knowledge in the four ways mentioned above, I strongly suspect that the grace of God does indeed build upon a natural psychic capacity. If Bohm is correct, reality is like the internet where everyone and everything is interconnected. It appears that psychic people can, with the Spirit's help, pick up random bits of information which are in the system. Speaking for myself, I have had precognitions of a non-religious kind on more than one occasion, e.g. when I knew for certain in October 1977 that the actor Charlie Chaplin would die on Christmas day of that year. I had told a number of people about my premonition. A skeptic could argue that, no matter what I felt, Chaplain's actual death on the nominated day was merely a coincidence. As for myself, I was quite sure that it was an instance of precognition. Over the years, I have suspected that the Lord has used that natural psychic sensitivity to enable me to have prophetic words of knowledge of a more spiritual kind, e.g. at healing services. An analogy is in order here. The church has distinguished between natural dreams that originate in the psyche, and religious dreams which originate in the human spirit as a result of the action of the Holy Spirit. Just as a religious dream is a letter written by God in the chamber of the human spirit upon paper supplied by the psyche, so a prophetic word of knowledge is dictated by God in the chamber of the spirit with the secretarial help of the psyche's extra-sensory powers.

Christian theology is opposed to all occult forms of knowledge. For example, the *Catechism of the Catholic Church* says in par 2116: 'All forms of divination are to be rejected ... consulting horoscopes, astrology, palm reading, interpretation of omens and lots ... the phenomenon of clairvoyance, and recourse to mediums all conceal for a desire for power over time, history and, in the last analysis, other human beings, as well as a wish to conciliate hidden powers.' When one reads this paragraph carefully, it becomes clear that the church isn't against clairvoyance as such, but against the abuse of this ability in an attempt to move away from reliance on divine providence.

Conclusion

The utterance of the prophetic word of knowledge is one of the more unusual and controversial gifts exercised by Pentecostal and Charismatic Christians. In most cases it seems to be the outcome of psychic sensitivity and divine inspiration. Because of the ever present danger of illusions and false inspirations, it is important to exercise discernment of spirits in order to ascertain whether prophetic words of knowledge, one's own or those of others, truly come from God (cf 1 Jn 4:1).

CHAPTER SIX

The Paranormal and Spirituality

As a result of public exposure on the media, I have received letters and phone calls from people all over Ireland who were frightened because of strange happenings, principally in their homes and workplaces. They ranged from footsteps, sounds of crying, smells, and objects moving, to electrical appliances going on and off. Some of them had been so terrified by what was happening that they had left their homes. Not surprisingly, they asked me to help. Usually I encouraged them to talk to their local clergy. Most of them would respond by saying that they had already done so. They would go on to recount how the priests they had spoken to had either dismissed their stories in a skeptical manner; said Mass or prayers in the house, often without any discernible effect; admitted that they were not competent to help; or referred them to me.

Enquiries of this kind prompted me, with a certain degree of reluctance, to become interested in this esoteric area of ministry. I read what I could, talked to others, reflected and prayed. Over the years I have became a little clearer about what might be involved in these problematic cases. The first thing I began to appreciate was the fact that a person's attitude to the strange phenomena in question is influenced by his or her worldview.

Worldviews

A worldview can be described as a set of presuppositions or assumptions which are held, either consciously or unconsciously, about the basic make-up of our world. It is arguable that currently there are three of them. Firstly, at one end of the spectrum of belief, there is a naturalistic worldview. It can be traced back to the Enlightenment. It denies the existence of the supernatural realm of God, good and evil spirits, heaven, hell, miracles and extrasensory experiences. It explains them away as mere myths that have no realistic substance. They are childish illusions that should be renounced in our scientific age.

Secondly, at the other end of the spectrum of belief, there is a supernatural worldview. For Christians it can be traced back to the scriptures. It acknowledges the other-worldly realm of God, good and evil spirits, heaven, hell, miracles and extrasensory experiences. Although its beliefs may be expressed in mythological language, that does not mean they are untrue. Myths are symbolic stories that encapsulate something of the indefinable mystery of God which cannot be fully grasped or expressed by the rational mind. Those who accept the existence of such a realm, also believe that God can and does reveal the divine presence, word and will to receptive people in both rational and pre-rational ways such as dreams, prophecy, visions etc.

Thirdly, there is a midway point on the spectrum between naturalistic and supernatural belief. It is adopted by many contemporary Christians, especially in the developed world. They espouse a liberal, more secularised worldview. While they accept basic beliefs such as the existence of God and the prospect of an after life, they are skeptical about the existence of many supernatural realities such as hell, angels, miracles, healings, exorcism etc. They don't really believe in the possibility of a pre-rational or extrasensory forms of communication with God.

In my experience there is an increasing number of people in Ireland, including some clergy, who, for all intents and purposes, adopt either a naturalistic or liberal point of view. To a greater or lesser extent they tend to be reductionist and explain away transcendental phenomena by saying, 'it is nothing but ...' For instance, they would try to interpret, the strange house disturbances already described, in either materialistic or psychological terms. It is only those who adopt a supernatural perspective that are likely to be truly sympathetic to those who seek help. I should say in passing that, although I use words like natural and supernatural, I believe that in reality they are intimately inter-woven. How this is so is a crucial theological point which will not be discussed here. Suffice it to say that Karl Rahner has de-scribed the supernatural or supernature as a participation in the meaning and life of God, which absolutely exceeds the powers and claims of any created spiritual nature.[1]

Normal and Paranormal Experience

Many of those who adopt the supernatural worldview believe that there are three interrelated realms that can be involved in disturbed dwellings.

a) Normal

Firstly, there is the material world which is governed by natural laws as described by empirical science. Quite often disturbances in a house will have a perfectly ordinary explanation such as creaking pipes or electrical faults, which are often misinterpreted by an overheated imagination. For instance, I visited a widow's home some time ago. She was frightened and felt that there was some sort of evil spirit active in her upstairs rooms. Quite frankly, when I chatted with her, I felt that she was interpreting every little sound as evidence of an alien presence. I reassured her, said a prayer for peace of mind, and as far as I know she has had no more trouble. Some time ago Fr Michael Nolan, a former lecturer in the philosophy department of University College Dublin, told me in an unsolicited latter that both he and the late Fr E. F. O' Doherty, Professor of Psychology in the same univer-sity, used to investigate disturbed homes. Fr Nolan said that neither he or his colleague ever came across a case that could not be explained in terms of natural causes. Having read his paper which contains many interesting case studies, I couldn't help thinking that the two men had adopted an *a priori* attitude that presumed that any explanation had to be a natural one. In other

---

1. Karl Rahner & Herbert Vorgrimler, 'Supernatural,' *Theological Dictionary* (New York: Herder & Herder, 1968), 450.

words, they seemed to be adopting either a naturalistic or liberal point of view.

This impression was confirmed when I read 'Psycho-pathology and Mystical Phenomena' in Professor O' Doherty's book *Psychology and Religion*.[2] This chapter makes his position very clear. Speaking about the devil and the possibility of possession he said: 'Belief in the occurrence of diabolical possession, obsession and similar so-called 'preternatural' manifestations can be ruled out.'[3] What surprises me about this assertion is that it owes more to reductionist science that to the teaching of scripture or the church, which has an official Rite of Exorcism, one which was revised in 1999. When he came to deal with the subject of extrasensory perception he said, that 'belief in this is a failure of reason and faith.'[4] He dismissed the possibility of telekinesis, i.e. the ability of the mind to influence the material world, as 'physically impossible'[5] and when he asked, 'Are there ghosts, are there poltergeists?' he answered emphatically, 'certainly not!'[6] Professor O' Doherty quoted a sociological maxim with approval: 'If men define situations as real, they are real in their consequences.'[7] In other words if you think there are fairies at the bottom of the garden you will probably find evidence of their presence. Is that necessarily true? While there can be some truth in the maxim, in the sense that our beliefs about ourselves and others can be self-fulfilling prophecies, it fails to accept that some of the situations that are defined as being real, are in fact real. It would seem that Professor O' Doherty was operating out of the opposite maxim: 'If men define situations as unreal, they are unreal in their consequences.' Tell that to someone whose house is disturbed, will it make the consequences disappear? If only it would.

---

2. Cf E. F. O' Doherty, *Religion and Psychology* (New York: Alba House, 1977)
3. *Religion and Psychology*, op. cit., 99.
4. *Religion and Psychology*, op. cit., 104.
5. *Religion and Psychology*, op. cit., 104.
6. *Religion and Psychology*, op. cit., 109
7. *Religion and Psychology*, op. cit., 106.

b) Paranormal

Then there is the natural but paranormal realm, sometimes referred to as Psi. The word paranormal is applied to observed phenomena or powers of extrasensory perception (ESP) which are presumed to operate beyond or outside those considered normal or known. Paranormal phenomena can be divided into three main classes:

1) Mental phenomena: unusual mental states or abilities, such as:
- Telepathy, mind to mind communication without any communication through normal sensory channels.
- Clairvoyance, being aware of distant objects and events without the participation of the senses. Nowadays, it is also referred to as anomalous cognition (i.e. unusual or exceptional forms of thinking).
- Precognition is extrasensory awareness of a future event.

2) Physical phenomena: unusual physical occurrences that may be controlled by consciousness, such as:
- Psychokinesis which refers to mental influence over objects.
- Poltergeists, noisy spirits.
- Stigmata, appearing to have the wounds of Christ in one's hands and/or feet.
- Materialisations, appearances of objects as if a hologram.
- Physical phenomena, unusual events not controlled by consciousness.
- Out of body experiences (OBEs), consciousness outside the body, e.g. seeing one's unconscious body in the operating theatre.
- Near death experiences (NDEs).

Paranormal phenomena are studied by parapsychologists, e.g. at the Rhine Institute at Duke University in the US and The Department of Parapsychology in Edinburgh University. However, it has to be said that parapsychological research does not have wide acceptance within the mainstream, scientific community. Many scientists maintain that parapsychological experiments are usually poorly designed and often lack proper controls which leaves room for intentional or unintentional information leakage through normal means. Furthermore, parapsychological experiments are rarely replicated with positive results at independent laboratories. Richard Broughton, director of research at the Institute of Parapsychology in Durham, North Carolina explains why some scientists may be slow to accept evidence that supports ESP: 'If the claims of parapsychology are correct then the existing worldview that science gives us will have to be modified – the so-called laws of physics will have to be re-written. Of itself this should not be controversial.'[8]

By and large mainline psychology either ignores ESP or says that there is little or no evidence that it is real. In his autobiography, Carl Jung stated that these reactions were due to the fact that: 'Rationalists insist to this day that parapsychological experiences do not really exist; for their worldview stands or falls on this question.'[9] Sir Alister Hardy said something similar when he wrote: 'If experimental scientific evidence for the existence of telepathy could be established, I believe that it would help people to accept a spiritual philosophy which is greatly needed in our materialistic society; it would show that there was a mental extension of the individual's psyche beyond the physio-chemical structure of the brain and so would lend plausibility to the concept of there being a spiritual dimension outside the strictly physical material world.'[10]

Arch-skeptic, James Randi, maintains that there is so little empirical evidence to indicate that paranormal activity is real, that he has offered a prize of one million dollars to anyone who can prove in a definitive way that the paranormal is authentic. I don't know what Randi makes of research done by the National Aeronautical Space Administration's investigation of clairvoyance. The American government gave NASA about $25 million to finance the Stargate project between 1970-1994. It investigated

---

8. *Parapsychology* (New York: Ballantine, 1991)
9. *Memories, Dreams, Reflections* (London: Fontana, 172), 335-336.
10. *The Spiritual Nature of Man: A Study of Contemporary Religious Experience* (Oxford: Oxford University Press, 1983), 44.

the phenomenon of anomalous cognition. The research, conducted under the most exacting scientific standards found that clairvoyance was a fact. It said that the odds against the findings being due to mere chance were one in a hundred billion, billion. In *Psychology, Religion and Spirituality*,[11] David Fontana draws attention to the fact that Professor Jessica Utts wrote in her conclusion to the Stargate report: 'It is clear that anomalous cognition is possible and has been demonstrated. This conclusion is not based on belief, but rather on commonly accepted scientific criteria.'[12] It appears, therefore, that at least one instance of paranormal activity has been substantiated in a scientific way.

For his part, sociologist Fr Andrew Greeley has studied surveys and polls since 1978, and has found that not only has the percentage of Americans admitting to psychic experiences increased, but about two thirds of college professors accept the phenomenon of extrasensory perception (ESP), and more than 25% of 'elite scientists' believe in ESP. Other polls have shown that many scientists hold such beliefs privately but do not publicly share such opinions for fear of ridicule. It would also be true to say that when researchers such as Hardy and Hood investigated the incidence of religious experience, many of the respondents reported occurrences that were paranormal in nature.

Catholic theology has taken some interest in this area if for no other reason than that many of the saints were associated with paranormal phenomena such as levitation, the odour of sanctity, and incorrupt bodies. For example, in the eighteenth century the immensely learned Pope Benedict XIV (1675-1758) wrote a four volume treatise *On the Beatification of the Servants of God, and the Canonization of the Blessed*. As was noted in the chapter on the prophetic word of knowledge, Pope Benedict XIV took a keen interest in parapsychological phenomena such as telepathy, clairvoyance and precognition and psychokinesis. He

---

11. (Oxford: BPS Blackwell, 2003).
12. Quoted in R. Hyman's 'Evaluation of a program on anomalous mental phenomena', *Journal of Scientific Exploration*, no 10, p 30.

noticed that they were not necessarily a sign of sanctity. However, he also recognised, as others have done since, notably theologian Karl Rahner,[13] that when grace was truly at work, these natural, but unusual, psychic abilities can be involved in many types of mystical experience such as apparitions and prophecies. So Catholicism is not opposed to parapsychological activities in spite of the fact that they are sometimes connected with divination or the occult. Karl Rahner believed that, far from being a bad thing, parapsychological investigation was important for a complete and detailed appreciation of how nature and grace may conspire to reveal God's care for humankind.

Poltergeists and Psychokinesis

Whereas in the past poltergeists (literally, 'noisy spirits') were considered to be the result of the activity of the spirits of the dead, modern researchers are fairly convinced that they are, more often than not, due to paranormal causes.[14] As such they have nothing to do with religion. Typically they are associated with thumps and bumps. Electrical appliances may go on and off, crockery may be thrown about the place or break into tiny bits. These phenomena may be caused by a type of uncontrolled psychokinesis. Parapsychologist, William G. Roll, has suggested that this phenomenon should be referred to as Recurrent Spontaneous Psychokinesis (RSPK). Poltergeist activity tends to be associated with a single person called an agent or a focus. Two-thirds of poltergeist disturbances have been traced to disturbed teenagers and the rest to adults who are emotionally upset. For example, I know one family where poltergeist activity was at its worst when a particular daughter, of about twenty, was having her period. When she left the house the poltergeist activity ended. By the way, the noises didn't bother the young woman at all.

Almost seventy years of research by the Rhine Research

---

13. Cf *Visions and Prophecies* (New York: Herder & Herder, 1963).
14. Cf Lisa Schwebel, *Apparitions, Healings and Weeping Madonnas: Christianity and the Paranormal* (New York: Paulist Press, 2004).

Center in the USA has led to the hypothesis among parapsychologists that the 'poltergeist effect' is a form of psychokinesis generated by a living, human mind. The 'poltergeist effect' may be
the outward manifestation of a psychological trauma suffered
by someone in the past. One study of poltergeist activity found
that 41% of the incidences were associated with people who had
problems in their homes. 15% of this segment of people were
known to have suffered from an emotional or mental problem
prior to the house disturbance. I have found that when one is
dealing with a case like this, it is good to encourage the people
involved to sort out their emotional and spiritual problems with
God's help, in the belief that when they are at peace the poltergeist activity will tend to cease. It is important to appreciate two
things when the paranormal is the main reason for disturbances
in dwellings. Firstly, it seems as if it is a natural occurrence.
Secondly, it is usually related to the psychic sensitivities and
abilities of the householders, which may be active in an unconscious way. Talking about poltergeist activity, Bishop Hugh
Montefiore says that although they are very upsetting they
should not be regarded as hauntings. So 'attempts to solve the
problem by releasing or expelling spirits is useless, indeed,
sometimes it aggravates the problem. Exorcism should not be
carried out, nor any ecclesiastical or other rite.'[15] He says, quite
rightly I think, that poltergeist activity doesn't harm people or
usually last for a long time.

The Restless Dead
Homes and other buildings can be haunted. People in those
dwellings can sense a presence. Sometimes they will see a ghostly
apparition. In a classic book entitled *Apparitions*, G. N. M. Tyrell
suggests that there are four different kinds:[16]
  • The first is what he calls experimental apparitions. In these
    cases a person deliberately projects his or her image into an-

---

15. *The Paranormal: A Bishop Investigates* (Leicestershire: Upfront, 2002),
88.
16. (London: Duckworth & Co., 1942).

other situation, e.g. where a person is in need. The recorded phenomenon of bi-location by Padre Pio in Italy and Sai Baba in India, would be examples.

- The second type of presence is that of crisis apparitions. In these a person sees a relative or friend at a time of crisis in that person's life such as extreme illness, an accident or the moment of death.

- The third category is that of postmortem apparitions where a person is known to be recently deceased, appears to the living.

- The fourth kind is referred to as a haunting or recurrent ghostly apparition which may be associated with poltergeist activity. This is the one that interests us most in this chapter. Firstly, let's look at an historical example. In his biography of John Wesley, Roy Hattersley recounts how, during his childhood, his home was haunted between December 1716 and February of the following year.[17] During that time the Wesleys believed that it was the ghost of a local man who had committed suicide. He was liable to appear during the night and the day. His visitations were associated with all kinds of noises. As soon as the family saw the ghost as nuisance more than a threat, the haunting ended without any prayers of exorcism having being said. On the basis of the evidence there is reason to believe that this was a paranormal occurrence of the poltergeist variety. It is worth noting that young people were living in the house. Perhaps one of them was a focal agent, so to speak, who was unwittingly connected with the disturbances.

Currently we are interested in the fourth kind of apparition described by Tyrell. If people are asked, 'Have you ever felt that you were in touch with someone who had died?' a Gallup poll in the USA indicated that 24% of the population thought that contact with the dead was possible.[18] Researchers, Kalish and

17. *John Wesley: A Brand from the Burning* (London: Abacus, 2002), 35-37.
18. Hood, Spilka, Hunsberger, Gorsuch, *The Psychology of Religion: An Empirical Approach* (New York: Guilford, 1996), 249.

Reynolds found that when they interviewed people about this subject as many as 40% claimed to have had contact with a deceased individual. What one is to make of these claims is hard to know.

a) A Psychic Imprint

There is circumstantial evidence which indicates that houses can be haunted by ghosts. One theory suggests that a ghost gets its energy from a location such as a house, a graveyard, or an old site. Such an imprint can, it seems, gain strength by repetition. Martin Israel, a Church of England priest, psychiatrist and exorcist says in his book *Exorcism: The Removal of Evil Influences* that ghosts are: 'are non-material deposits of obsessional material that have arisen from past experiences of people who have dwelt in a particular place ... the unquiet dead can also appear as ghosts, but in this situation they show their independent personalities, making their emotional responses very obvious.'[19] In other words if something terrible or traumatic had taken place in that locality, one which involved strong, turbulent emotions, there might be some kind of psychic imprint in the local environment. It might be that psychically sensitive people would be able to decode the imprint in an auditory or imaginative way. The location where such an event took place is often oppressive, especially to people who are psychically sensitive.

b) Earthbound Spirits

There is reason to think that it is possible that when a person dies, he or she may be reluctant to leave their worldly dwelling place. Their spirit, therefore, is earthbound. So s/he haunts the area they were familiar with during life. If I'm consulted about a haunting, I encourage the people in the disturbed house or building to try and find out who the disturbed soul might be. Sometimes discrete enquiries in the neighbourhood leads to relevant information. In my experience, it is often about someone who suffered some kind of injustice or violence in that location.

---

19. (London: SPCK, 1999).

For example, I visited one house where the whimper of a baby was often heard. Then by chance the family heard that a baby had been abused there, years before they bought the house. The restless spirit may give the impression of being either playful, resentful, or angry. One can pray in the house, urging the restless soul to move on to meet with a loving and merciful God while praying, if need be, that the Lord would forgive the perpetrator for his or her wrongdoing. I'm sure that Bishop Montefiore is correct when he says that the eucharist should be offered on the departed soul's behalf.

There is a distinct but related dimension to this subject which is worth mentioning. In his book *Healing the Family Tree*,[20] Dr Kenneth McCall, a Protestant psychiatrist, made the surprising suggestion that requiem Mass should be celebrated for restless souls, while commending them to God. McCall believes that such spirits can exercise a negative influence on family members, e.g. by causing one of them to become anorexic. For instance, when I said Mass for the souls of deceased relatives in one home, a daughter, who had been depriving herself of food for about seven years, recovered completely.

Exorcising Places
Whether we believe in the existence of the devil or not, most of us are familiar with the notion of exorcism, where a priest appointed by the bishop prays for someone who is thought to be possessed. However, many people may not be familiar with the notion that a place can be influenced by an evil spirit and that it would need to be exorcised by means of a cleansing prayer. In his helpful book *Deliverance from Evil Spirits: A Manual*[21] Francis Mc Nutt suggests that there can be three reasons for demonic influence in a place:
1) When it has been targeted by curses, hexes or spells by satanic groups, which would be very rare.
2) When crimes or other serious sins have been committed

20. (London: Sheldon Press, 1994)
21. (London: Hodder & Stoughton, 1996), 289.

there, e.g. gross sexual behaviour, involvement with the occult such as using the Ouija board, or black magic may have
been practised there in the recent or distant past.

3) When demonised people have lived in or spent time visiting
the place.

I may say in passing that such an evil spirit may oppress one
of the people in the house because of some psycho-spiritual vulnerability, e.g. as a result of involvement with the occult, abuse
in childhood, or deliberate involvement in serious sin, e.g. violent activity as a member of a paramilitary organisation. There
are tell-tale signs of negative infestations, such as inexplicable
coldness or a bad smell. As a *Would You Believe* programme on
RTÉ indicated in 2005, I assisted, Canon Billy Lendrum, a
Church of Ireland minister[22] with a such case in Northern
Ireland, where it was claimed that holy water boiled, a prayer to
Michael the Archangel spontaneously went on fire, and a rosary
and other religious objects were flung on the floor. Although
these events could be seen as the result of poltergeist activity, we
felt, rightly or wrongly, that it might have been due to infestation by an evil spirit. Following careful discernment, a prayer
of simple exorcism was said, in order to rid the area of the evil
influence and to invoke God's blessing upon it in the future.
Thank God it was effective at the time and the couple moved
back into their home. I have found that it can be helpful if such
prayer is accompanied by the use of either blessed salt or holy
water which is sprinkled in the room/s. As a result of spiritual
discernment it may also be necessary to pray for deliverance
and/or inner healing for one of the people living in the house.

Exorcising People
While the clergy should help people with house disturbances,
the scriptures clearly indicate, that exorcism of people is a prior-
ity (Cf Mk 16:17).[23] Christians distinguish between obsession

22. Cf Billy Lendrum, *Confronting the Paranormal: A Christian Perspective*
(Belfast: Edenderry Print, 2001).
23. Cf Pat Collins 'Exorcism and the Falling Phenomenon', *Maturing in
the Spirit* (Dublin: Columba, 1981), 141-156; 'Faith and Deliverance

and possession by evil spirits. When people are obsessed, they suffer from a sort of spiritual neurosis where only part of their personality is subject to demonic influence. As I know from experience, obsessed people need a simple exorcism which can be prayed by any faith-filled believer. For instance, I can remember praying, a number of years ago, for a twelve year old girl who had been involved in the occult. I asked the Spirit of God to free her from a morbid spirit of divination. Thankfully, it was effective and she experienced inner peace from then onwards.

When people are possessed, they suffer from a form of spiritual psychosis because the devil seems to take over their entire personalities, if not permanently, then for periods of time. As a result they can have extraordinary physical strength which is inconsistent with their age or state of health. They may also have an ability to speak unknown languages and to discern hidden and distant things. I have never met a possessed person over a 30 year period. The vast majority of the bizarre behaviours I have come across can be explained in medical and psychiatric ways, e.g. schizophrenia, epilepsy or Tourette's syndrome. When the Vatican published its *New Rite of Exorcism* in 1999 it stated clearly that the majority of the cases that present as cases needing exorcism can be explained in psychological ways. Fr de Tonquedoc, a well known French exorcist echoed this point of view when he wrote: 'Address the devil, and you will see him, or rather, not him but a portrait made up of the sick person's ideas of him.'[24] The small percentage of truly possessed people need solemn exorcism by a priest who has been officially appointed for that purpose by the bishop. Films like *The Exorcism of*

From Evil', *Finding Faith in Troubled Times* (Dublin: Columba, 1993), 102-147; *Unveiling The Heart: How to Overcome Evil in the Christian Life* (Dublin: Veritas, 1995); 'Spiritual Warfare', *Spirituality for the 21st Century* (Dublin: Columba, 1999), 170-179; 'Atheism and the Father of Lies', *The Broken Image* (Dublin: Columba, 2002), 208-220; Dara de Faoite, 'Spirit Forces', *Paranormal Ireland* (Ashbourne: Maverick, 2002), 67-83.
24. *Les Maladies Nerveuses ou Mentales et les Manifestations Diaboliques* (Paris: Beauchesne, 1938).

Emily Rose (2005), do not give an accurate idea of what an exorcism is really like. They tend to be overly dramatic. Speaking on the basis of my own limited experience, Frank Mc Nutt gives a more accurate picture of what a typical exorcism is like in chapter thirteen of his book *Deliverance from Evil Spirits: A Manual*.[25] However, it is true that on occasion the person in need of deliverance may have telepathic knowledge and abnormal strength.

Those who engage in this ministry learn a number of points through experience. They prepare by prayer and fasting. They confess their sins to God and receive forgiveness. Catholics can do this in the sacrament of reconciliation. People unknown to the priest should not be present. If he is praying for a woman, another woman should be present, if possible. The unconscious imagery should not be that of the lover, but rather that of caring parents. Animals and children shouldn't be present during the time of ministry.

Conclusion

As you can see from these brief observations, house disturbances can be due to a number of causes. Those who want to deal with them effectively need to be *au fait* with psychology, the paranormal, the notion of the restless dead, and the possibility of infestation by evil. Like good doctors, they diagnose what the nature of the problem is, and then try to come up with an appropriate remedy. I may say in passing that Occam's Razor should be used in all cases, i.e. for purposes of explanation things not known to exist should not, unless it is absolutely necessary, be postulated as existing. Not all priests would be expected to know about such things, any more than all doctors would be expected to know all about rare diseases. Good doctors refer difficult medical cases to specialists. Surely, priests should be able to refer difficult cases, to do with such things as poltergeists, hauntings and demonic infestation, to diocesan specialists. Otherwise those who are afflicted may be tempted to have re-

---

25. Op. cit., 179-195.

course to New Age practitioners, spiritualists, psychics and other non-Christian helpers.

For some time now I have felt that there was need for a forum which would explore this controversial area with the help of such people as theologians, psychologists, parapsychologists, and experienced exorcists. Study and discussion of this kind would aim to explore this aspect of ministry with a view to increasing experiential knowledge and forming an association of experts both clerical and lay. There is a precedent in the Church of England. In 1972 the Bishop of Exeter set up such a body. In 1975 the bishops released a report which contained guidelines for exorcism. In the meantime most Church of England dioceses have appointed exorcists whose main task is to deal with poltergeists and hauntings and to comfort those who are upset by paranormal phenomena.[26] Arguably, the Catholic Church in Ireland needs to do something similar. To do so would accord with canon 1172 of *The Code of Canon Law*. Exorcists could be been trained to deal not only with disturbed buildings but also with people who are oppressed by evil. It is worth noting that, in early 2005, the Legionaries of Christ initiated a course on exorcism in their Regina Apostolorum University, in Rome. Like the course participants, all of us can ask in the words of a Cornish prayer: 'From ghoulies and ghosties and long legged besties and things that go bump in the night, Good Lord, deliver us.'

---

26. *The Paranormal: A Bishop Investigates*, op. cit., 114-115.

CHAPTER SEVEN

Childhood Experiences and Atheism

I think it would be true to say that up to 300 years ago societies everywhere tended to be religious and to believe either in God or Gods. As the psalmist observed, 'only the fool says in his heart, "there is no God"' (Ps 53:1). Of course there were always exceptions, theoretical or practical atheists who either acted as if God did not exist or who, for one reason or another, denied the existence of a Supreme Being. I have long believed that atheism is one of the key spiritual problems of our times. I was encouraged to find that not only did the *General Catechetical Directory* state in par 7 that 'atheism must be regarded as one of the most serious problems of our time,'[1] Pope John Paul II also held this same belief. He was worried by the fact that, ever since the Enlightenment in the eighteenth century, increasing numbers of people in the secularised cultures of the West, especially in Europe, had become forgetful of God. Western culture, he observed, "gives the impression of silent apostasy on the part of people who have all that they need and who live as if God does not exist.'[2] The fact that the proposed constitution of the EU didn't mention God seemed to confirm this observation.

In his encyclical, *Lord and Giver of Life* (1986) Pope John Paul II argued that the agnosticism and atheism, which are so prevalent, are ultimately due to the illusions and false inspirations of the devil, the father of lies. He wrote: 'Satan manages to sow in man's soul the seed of opposition to the One who, from the beginning, would be considered as man's enemy, and not as

---

1. *Vatican Council II: More Post Conciliar Documents*, ed. Austin Flannery, (Dublin: Dominican Publications, 1982), 534.
2. John Paul II, *Ecclesia in Europa* (2003), par. 9

Father. Man is challenged to become the adversary of God!'[3] Later in the same paragraph he added: 'through the influence of the father of lies ... there will be a constant pressure on man to reject God, even to the point of hating him.' It seems fairly obvious that John Paul had the writings of a number of notable atheists such as Auguste Comte, Karl Marx, Friedrich Nietzsche, Ludwig Feuerbach and Sigmund Freud in mind when he made this statement. John Paul believed that rejection of God would have dire effects. Here are four he mentioned.

Firstly, people would lose touch with their deeper spiritual selves. John Paul strongly believed that whereas we get to know our psychic selves in and through relationship with other people and the world about us, we get to know our spiritual selves through relationship with God, whose mystery is mediated to us in and through our relationship with people and the world. The Holy Father reiterated this psychological and spiritual truth in a number of his encyclicals. Here are just three typical examples. In par 8 of *Splendour of the Truth* (1993) he wrote: 'The man who wishes to understand himself thoroughly ... must, so to speak, enter Christ with all his own self; he must appropriate and assimilate the whole of the reality of the incarnation and redemption in order to find himself.' In par 23 of *The New Millenium* (2001), the Pope maintained that contemplating the face of Christ has the effect of 'fully revealing man to man himself.' In par 25 of *The Rosary of the Virgin Mary* (2002) he said: 'Anyone who contemplates Christ through the various stages of his life cannot fail to perceive in him the truth about man. This is the great affirmation of the Second Vatican Council which I have so often discussed in my own teaching since the Encyclical letter *Redemptor Hominis* (1979): it is only in the mystery of the Word made flesh that the mystery of man is seen in its true light.' In other words, if you want to know *who* you are, you need to know *whose* you are. Absence from God means absence from one's deepest spiritual self.

---

3. Par 38.

Secondly, John Paul II believed that, not surprisingly, absence from God would lead to the apparent silence of God. John Paul said shortly before his death: 'Isn't existential solitude the result of deserting God and perhaps the profound source of *all* (my italics) the dissatisfaction we perceive in our day? So much insecurity, so many thoughtless reactions originate in our having abandoned God, the rock of our salvation.' By the way, the Pope did not believe that God was withdrawing the divine presence from our sinful world, and threatening it with retributive punishment, as the Italian press mistakenly suggested in 2002. As was noted in the introduction to this book, it is self-centred people who are withdrawing from God.

Thirdly, John Paul felt that unbelief leads to *openness to demonic influences*. There is reason to suspect that when people are alienated from God and, therefore, their deepest selves, they are particularly vulnerable to the perverted and perverting activities of the devil who is referred to in scripture as the 'prince of this world' (Jn 12:31; 14:30; 16:11). As he secretly exploits the unacknowledged darkness of the human heart (cf Jer 17:9) and the unjust structures of society, he seeks to carry out his devious and destructive purposes (cf Jn 8:44). As was made clear at the launch of the church's *Revised Rite of Exorcism*, because of the devil's insidious activity, individual people, communities and whole societies can be caught up in enormous splurges of evil such as the violence of the Second Word War, the spread of pornography, child sex abuse, political corruption and the drugs trade. Although, historians may describe the causes of problems, like these, in merely human terms, the Pope suspects that in some mysterious way, that is beyond the grasp of intellectual understanding, they are ultimately expressions of a pathology of evil that is stirred up by the evil One who initiates his evil tactics by first separating people from God.

Fourthly, lack of faith in God leads to the *culture of death and hopeless solitude*. John Paul has also spoken about some of the likely consequences of alienation from God: 'It makes it possible,' he said, 'to erase from the countenance of men and women

the marks of their likeness to God and thus lead them little by little either to *a destructive will to power or to a solitude without hope*
(My italics).' The destructive will to power, mentioned by John
Paul II, is evident in what he referred to as 'the culture of death.'
It can, and does find expression in evils such as abortion, so
called mercy killings, capital punishment, terrorist murders of
innocent people and genocide. The solitude without hope John
Paul referred to, is also quite evident in modern culture. Psychiatrists say that instead of enjoying a sense of ultimate belonging, many people are afflicted by an anxious sense of meaning-
lessness. He has said that, as a consequence: 'a vast field has
opened up for the unrestrained development of nihilism in philosophy, relativism in values and morality and even cynical
hedonism in daily life.'[4] Many people espouse an *à la carte* approach to morality especially in the areas of sex and business. In
this regard one is reminded of the last verse in the Book of
Judges: 'In those days there was no king in Israel; all the people
did what was right in their own eyes' (Jdg 21:25).

Psychology's contribution to contemporary Atheism
Arguably, Ludwig Feuerbach was the father of modern atheism.
The son of a famous jurist, he was born in Landshut, in South
East Germany. He studied theology at Heidelberg and Berlin,
then philosophy at Erlangen. He was a pupil of Hegel, but eventually reacted against his idealism. Feuerbach's most famous
work, was *The Essence of Christianity* (1841). It was translated into
English by the novelist George Eliot. Writing about his aim he
said: 'The task I set myself ... was to transform friends of God
into friends of man, believers into thinkers, devotees of prayer
into devotees of work, candidates for the hereafter into students
of this world, Christians who, by their own profession and admission, are "half animal, half angel," into men, into whole
men.'[5] He wanted to do this because he claimed that theistic religion alienated human beings from their deepest selves and their

4. *Ecclesia in Europa*, par 9.
5. End of Lecture XXX, *Lectures on the Essence of Religion*.

true potential by projecting their attributes, powers and possibilities on to God. As Feuerbach wrote: 'To enrich God man must become poor, that God may be all, man must be nothing.'[6] The sooner people realised that self-alienation was the result of belief in a transcendent God, the sooner they could develop a humanistic religion. It is fascinating to see how Feuerbach took a number of qualities that were traditionally attributed to God and showed how they had human equivalents. In this way Feuerbach translated theology into anthropology. The historical course of religion he said, 'consists in this: that what by an earlier religion was regarded as objective, is now regarded as subjective; that is, what was formerly contemplated and worshipped as God is now perceived to be something human ... man's only God is man himself.'[7] Although this was ostensibly a philosophical argument,[8] it is quite obvious that it was expressed in a psychological way.

Feuerbach's book made a big impact on a number of nineteenth century thinkers, among them Engels, Marx, Wagner, Nietzsche, Frazier and Freud. Speaking about Feuerbach in 1875, Freud said: 'Among all philosophers, I worship and admire this man the most.'[9] It would probably be true to say that Freud expressed Feuerbach's philosophical theory in purely psychological terms. He said: 'All I have done – and this is the only thing which is new in my exposition – is to add some psychological foundation to the criticisms of my great predecessor.'[10] In *The Psychopathology of Everyday Life*, Freud wrote: 'One could venture to explain ... the myths of paradise and the fall of man, of God, of good and evil, of immortality, and so on, and *to transform metaphysics into meta-psychology*. (my italics)' He felt that it would lead to man's third great disillusionment. The first

---

6. *The Essence of Christianity*, op. cit., chap 1, sec 2.
7. Lecture XXX.
8. Feuerbach said of himself: 'I am nothing but an intellectual researcher into nature.'
9. Peter Gay' *Freud: A Life for our Time*, (London: Papermac, 1988), 28
10. *Kung's Freud and the Problem of God*, (New Haven: Yale University Press, 1979) 75.

was the cosmological one when Copernicus proposed the helio-centric view of the universe, the second was the biological one when Darwin proposed that man was descended from the apes. The third was the psychoanalytic one when Freud undermined the claims of rational consciousness by showing how the ir-rational unconscious, influences conscious behaviour while also indicating that belief in God and immortality was merely an in-fantile wish fulfillment.

Sigmund Freud

Freud maintained that religion had three main aims as far as be-lievers were concerned: 'It gives information about the origin and coming into existence of this universe, it assures them of its protection and of ultimate happiness in the ups and downs of life and it directs their thoughts and actions by precepts which it lays down with its whole authority.'[11] Speaking about the limit-ations of his own work, Freud said: 'To assess the truth value of religious doctrine does not lie within the scope of the present in-quiry. It is enough for us that we have recognised them as being, in their psychological nature, illusions.'[12] It is worth noting that Freud does not say that religious beliefs are delusions, i.e. false in themselves. As a scientist he wasn't in a position to pronounce on metaphysical matters. When he states that they are illusions, he is talking from a psychological rather than a philosophical point of view. Religious beliefs are illusions because he can demonstrate from a psychological perspective that they are wish fulfillments. It is possible that a belief which is considered to be an illusion from a psychological point of view could be true from a philosophical point of view. Nevertheless, it would be ac-curate to say, that while logically Freud would have accepted the distinction between illusion and delusion, because of his personal prejudices he actually regarded religious illusions as delusions.

Its worth mentioning in passing that British psychologist Donald Winnicot evaluates illusions in a more positive way

11. *New Introductory Lectures on Psycho-analysis.*
12. *The Future of an Illusion.*

than Freud. Both he and others have shown that children invest transitional objects such as blankets and teddy bears with feelings they have had for their mothers. Rather than being a bad thing, this it is a necessary and healthy stage in the weakening of the child's dependence on its mother and its growing autonomy as a separate person. Winnicot has suggested that religion is a transitional phenomenon, an illusion functioning in the intermediate space between inner and outer reality. He writes: 'The task of reality-acceptance is never completed ... No human being is free from the strain of relating inner and outer reality, and ... relief from this strain is provided by an intermediate area of experience which is not challenged – arts, *religion*, (my italics) etc.'[13] It is clear that Winnicot not only refuses to treat illusions, whether mundane or religious, as delusions, he sees that they can be good and necessary psychological ways of adapting to reality both in childhood and in adult life.

Religion as Neurosis

Freud's psychological theory of religion was most clearly and simply expressed in his book, *The Future of an Illusion*. As the title implies he believed that religion was a form of illusion, that is: 'fulfillments of the oldest, strongest and most urgent wishes of mankind.' He argued his case from two points of view, historical and personal.

a) The historical/mythical argument

Freud was influenced by Darwin's evolutionary perspective and by the writings of a number of men who examined the possible origins of the religious instinct, such as Robertson Smith and J. G. Frazer. He linked the notions of Totemism and the incest taboo as explanations of the childish and illusory origins of religion. In *Totem and Taboo*, he proposed a rather fanciful history of religious origins.[14] Ana-Maria Rizzuto includes a lucid and

---

13. *The Birth of the Living God: A Psychoanalytic Study*, op. cit., 179; cf W. W. Meissner SJ, MD, *Psychoanalysis and Religious Experience*, (New Haven: Yale University Press, 1984), 164-184.
14. Penguin Freud Library 13, *The Origins of Religion* (London: Penguin, 1985), 43-224.

helpful one-page summary of Freud's idiosyncratic views in her book *The Birth of the Living God: A Psychoanalytic Study*.[15] Freud applied the idea of the Oedipus complex – involving unresolved sexual feelings, e.g. a son desiring to have an exclusive erotic relationship with his mother accompanied by hostility toward his father – and postulated its emergence in the primordial stage of human development. This stage he conceived to be one in which there were small groups, each dominated by a father. According to Freud's reconstruction of primordial society, the father was displaced by a son (probably violently), and further attempts to displace the new leader brought about a truce in which incest taboos, i.e. proscriptions against sexual relations within the family, were formed. The slaying of a suitable animal, symbolic of the murdered father, connected totemism with taboo. In *Moses and Monotheism* Freud reconstructed biblical history in accord with his general theory.

Freud summarised his argument as follows: 'The father of the primal horde, since he was an unlimited despot, had seized all the women for himself; his sons, being dangerous to him as rivals, had been killed or driven away. One day, however, the sons came together and united to overwhelm, kill and devour their father, who had been their enemy but also their ideal. After the deed they were unable to take over their heritage since they stood in one another's way. Under the influence of failure and remorse they learned to come to an agreement among themselves; they banded themselves into a clan of brothers by the help of the ordinances of totemism, which aimed at preventing a repetition of such a deed, and they jointly undertook to forego the possession of the women on whose account they had killed their father. They were then driven to finding strange women, and this was the origin of the exogamy which is so closely bound up with totemism. The totem meal was the festival commemorating the fearful deed from which sprang man's sense of guilt and which was the beginning at once of social organisation, of religion and of ethical restrictions.'[16] In another place Freud

---

15. (Chicago: The University of Chicago Press, 1979), 24.

said: 'The primal crime of mankind must have been a parricide, the killing of the primal father of the primitive horde, *whose image was later transfigured into a deity.*'[17] (my italics)

There are a number of problems with Freud's retrospective application of the Oedipus complex. He began with a personal *a priori* assumption about the origin of the delusional belief in God and then tried to support it, in an arbitrary way, with ideas borrowed from the history of religion. Not surprisingly, ethnologists were critical of his views, as were historians and biblical scholars who argued that his account was neither in accord with the methods or findings of scholarship. Furthermore, his ideas didn't account for all religions, for example, Buddhism doesn't have a father figure to worship.

b) The Personal argument

Freud said that as babies we are helpless and depend on our parents for food, clothing and care. But as we grow older we assert our autonomy and independence. We no longer submit to the authority of our genetic father. But we live in a dangerous and threatening world. We are intimidated and constrained by the vagaries of nature, earthquakes, storms, floods, diseases and death, and by the inhibitions imposed upon us by culture, its various do's and don'ts which, in many instances, prevent us doing what we like. In order to cope with the nastiness and brutishness of life, people have a wish for a new protective and caring father. Freud argued that God the Father was a projection of that wish. He wrote: 'Psychoanalysis has made us familiar with the intimate connection between the father-complex and belief in God; it has shown us that a personal God is, psychologically speaking, nothing other than an exalted father ... Thus we recognise that the roots of the need for religion are in the parental complex.'[18]

16. From part IV of *Autobiographical Study* 1925, in H. Küng, *Freud and the Problem of God*, op. cit., 38-39.
17. Quoted by Rizutto, *The Birth of the Living God*, op. cit., 17.
18. Quoted by Rizutto, *The Birth of the Living God*, op. cit., 15.

In one of his earliest papers, 'Obsessive acts and Religious Practices' (1907), Freud stated his belief that religion was a universal, obsessional neurosis.[19] He believed that any neurosis was the result of repression, often of instinctual sexual feelings such as those involved in the Oedipus complex. Repression is the mechanism by which the mind prevents experiences and their associated feelings, from passing from the unconscious into consciousness. As a result there is a conflict between the conscious ego and the unconscious id (i.e. instinctual self), and it is this conflict that gives rise to neurotic disorders and obsessional behaviours such as compulsive hand washing. The feelings that have been disowned express themselves in neurotic symptoms. As an obsessional neurosis, religion is formed through the suppression of certain instinctual impulses, amongst which is the sexual instinct. Religion is thus the expression of the instincts it has suppressed. Not only did Freud reject religious belief, he also made it clear in a letter to Romain Rolland, a French author, that he rejected the notion of non-theistic spirituality of the mystical kind because it too was an escape from reality.[20]

A Counter argument

While he was by no means the only psychologist encouraging modern unbelief, Freud certainly contributed to that trend. As John Paul II has stated, modern atheistic humanism 'is an attempt to promote a vision of man apart from God and apart from Christ. This sort of thinking has led to man being considered as the absolute centre of reality, a view which makes him occupy – falsely – the place of God and which forgets that it is not man who creates God, but rather God who creates man.'[21] Although some atheistic psychologists, such as Fromm and Maslow, promote the notion of non-theistic spirituality, I'm con-

19. Sigmund Freud, *The Origins of Religion* (London: Penguin, 1990), 27-42.

20. *Freud: A Life For Our Time*, op. cit., 544; Michael Palmer, *Freud and Jung on Religion*, (London: Routledge, 1997), 37.

21. *Ecclesia in Europa*, par 9.

vinced that they are not only likely to be buffeted by the problems mentioned by John Paul II at the beginning of this chapter, but also by the dictatorship of relativism mentioned by Benedict XVI.

As the father of the atheistic trend in psychology, Freud's thinking is open to criticism on two levels, psychological and philosophical. We noted that Freud's illusion theory is rooted in Feuerbach's notion of projection. Freud was quite correct in saying that psychological factors influence people's idea of God. Religion can certainly be an illusion, the expression of unresolved conflicts in the personality. But it need not be so. But even if it could be demonstrated that every religious person on earth espoused religion as a way of escaping from the harsh realities of life, no logical philosophical conclusions about the existence, or non existence, of God can be drawn from this fact. As Hans Küng points out: 'The mere fact of projection does not decide the existence or nonexistence of the object to which it refers.'[22]

We saw that Freud used the oedipal complex to explain in historical terms why religion was a universal, obsessional neurosis. Commenting on this view, Mircea Eliade, one of the great scholars of religion in the twentieth century, has expressed surprise that Freud's *Totem and Taboo* could have been such an incredible success among Western intellectuals, when the leading ethnologists of Freud's own time, such as Rivers, Boas, Kroeber, Malinowski and Schmidt, had proved the absurdity of the notion of the totemic banquet. They had pointed out, apparently in vain, that totemism was not found at the beginning of religions. Eliade says that no matter how flawed Freud's mythical theory might have been, it established a fashion among those who were dissatisfied 'with the worn-out forms of historical Christianity and their desire to rid themselves of their forefather's faith.'[23]

---

22. *Freud and the Problem of God*, op. cit, 77- 78.
23. Quoted by Küng, *Freud and the Problem of God*, op. cit., 74.

Paul Vitz's Inversion of Freud's Thesis

A few years ago Professor Paul Vitz wrote an interesting article entitled 'The Psychology of Atheism.' It has since been expanded into a book entitled, *Faith of the Fatherless: The Psychology of Atheism.*[24] Vitz states, quite rightly, that there is a widespread assumption in Western countries that belief in God is based on all kinds of irrational and immature needs and wishes. However, in marked contrast, atheism is derived from a rational, no-nonsense appraisal of the way things really are. However, Vitz points out that Freud's projection theory is unsupported by either psychoanalytic theory or the kind of clinical evidence that would have been provided by a believing patient. For example, Michael Argyle refers to research done by Hartel and Donahue. They studied 3,400 members of families and found that, contrary to Freud's belief, God was seen as loving rather than as an authority figure by children, especially girls.[25]

Furthermore, Vitz says that Freud's critique of religious belief rested on the foundation stone of the questionable theory of the Oedipus complex. However, if one were to accept the validity of that theory, says Vitz, it could be used to show that atheism rather than belief is an illusion. In postulating a universal Oedipus complex as the origin of our neuroses, unbeknown to himself, Freud inadvertently developed a good reason for understanding the rejection of God as the result of an unconscious wish fulfillment. After all, the unconscious Oedipus complex, which develops in childhood, becomes the dominant motive for hating the father, and by extension God as a psychological equivalent of the father. It leads to a desire that he would cease to exist, a wish that is sometimes expressed in the boy's desire to replace or kill the father. Because Freud repeatedly asserted that God was the psychological equivalent of the father, it logically follows that a natural consequence of the Oedipus complex would be an unconscious desire that God would not exist. As a result, says Vitz: 'in the Freudian framework, atheism is an illus-

---

24. (Dallas: Spence Publishing Company, 1999).
25. *Psychology and Religion* (London: Routledge, 2000), 98-99.

ion caused by the Oedipal desire to kill the father (God) and replace him with oneself. To act as though God does not exist reveals a wish to kill him, much in the same way as in a dream the image of a parent going away or disappearing can represent such a wish. The belief that 'God is dead,' therefore, is simply an Oedipal wish fulfillment – the sign of seriously unresolved unconscious motivation.'[26]

Not only has Vitz come up with an ingenious inversion of Freud's argument, he goes on to say that there is considerable evidence to indicates that many of those who deny the existence of God had inadequate fathers. Their dads may have lost their authority because of moral weakness, cowardice or abuse of one kind or another. They may also have been emotionally or physically absent due to such things as egotism, mental illness, work, desertion or premature death. In his book, Vitz provides his readers with a long list of biographical sketches which seek to relate the atheistic stance of people such as Friedrich Nietzsche, David Hume, Bertrand Russell, Jean Paul Sartre, Albert Camus, Arthur Schopenhauer, and Ludwig Feuerbach to either dead, absent, abusive or weak fathers. For example, Feuerbach's father was not only volatile and impulsive, he had a volcanic temper. When he was nine years of age, Ludwig's dad had an adulterous, nine year long, affair with Nanette Brunner, a married woman. He left home, lived openly with his mistress in a nearby town, where they had a son called Anselm. When Nanette died it is surprising to find that he returned to his wife Wilhelmine! In like manner, Freud didn't have a good relationship with Jacob, his remote, disciplinarian father. He was a weak man unable to provide financially for his family. For example, when he experienced business difficulties the family had to move from Moravia to Vienna. Often the money needed to support the household seems to have been provided by his wife's family. Furthermore, Freud's father was passive whenever he experienced anti-Semitism. He recounted an occasion when Jacob didn't react when someone called him a dirty Jew and knocked off his hat.

---

26. *Faith of the Fatherless*, op. cit., 13.

Young Sigmund was mortified by his father's weakness. In two of his adult letters he implied that his father was a sexual pervert and that his own children were among his victims. Vitz would argue that, at an unconscious level, Sigmund Freud despised his father and wished he were dead. His denial of God's existence was linked to his hostility to his earthly father.

Anyone who reads Vitz's book might come to the conclusion that it has two weak points. Firstly, the author chooses to speak about atheists who had inadequate fathers, but fails to tell us whether there were atheists who had very good fathers. Secondly, he doesn't tell us whether inadequate mothering also inclines people toward unbelief. Abraham Maslow, a well known humanistic psychologist was a lifelong atheist. Admittedly, his relationship with his father was far from intimate. Abraham saw very little of him in childhood. His marriage was an unhappy one so he worked away from home a lot. He wrote in his diary, 'My father misunderstood me, thought me an idiot and a fool. Probably too, he was disappointed in me.'[27] I may say in passing that Abraham Maslow was no fool, he had an astounding IQ of 195! While he was distant from his father for many years, he always hated his mother. He described her in these shocking words: 'What I reacted against and totally hated and rejected was not only her physical appearance, but also her values and worldview, her stinginess, her total selfishness, her lack of love for anyone else in the world, even her own husband and children, her narcissism ... her assumption that anyone was wrong who disagreed with her, her lack of concern for her grandchildren, her lack of friends, her sloppiness and dirtiness, her lack of family feeling for her own parents and siblings, her primitive animal-like care for herself and her body alone etc. etc.'[28] Apparently, Maslow loathed his mother so much that he didn't even attend her funeral. I'd suspect that this lifelong resentment played a role in his denial of God's existence because, in the first

---

27. Edward Hoffman, *The Right to be Human: A Biography of Abraham Maslow* (Los Angeles, Crucible, 1989), 6.
28. *The Right to be Human*, op. cit., 9.

period of his life, a boy feels that he is at one with his mother, who, like a mirror, reflects the ultimate power, love and authority of God.[29] If he found his mother wanting, and rejected her, it is not surprising that he might reject God also.

If Vitz's thesis is correct, and in general terms I think it is, then it has worrying implication in the context of Western countries where there is such widespread marriage breakdown and a growing number of one parent families. Apart from all the emotional problems this can cause for children, there is a real possibility that the inadequacy or absence of effective fathering and mothering will lead to a growing incidence of unbelief. This has tragic consequences, because I'm convinced that religious teachers such as Thomas Merton and John Paul II were correct when they said that absence from God means absence from one's own deepest spiritual self and its potentials.

Conclusion

Freud's critique of religion has some good points in so far as it indicates that, instead of embracing reality, religion and spirituality can be used to escape it. In this connection one is reminded of Gerard Manley Hopkins's description of a nun: 'I have desired to go where springs not fail, to fields where flies no sharp and sided hail and a few lilies blow.' His thinking on the interrelationship of the id, ego and superego was not discussed here. However, is not only helpful in understanding the notion of neurotic guilt, it has important implications for the way in which people form images of God. Those with an unhealthy, overbearing superego (i.e. conscience) tend to relate to God as a distant, demanding, and punitive figure, whereas those who have a healthy superego tend to relate to God as benevolent, compassionate and kind. Beit-Hallahmi and Argyle have shown, in reviewing several empirical studies to test the hypo-

29. Cf. Nancy Chodorow, *The Reproduction of Mothering: Psychoanalysis and the Sociology of Gender*; Lillian Rubin, *Intimate Strangers: Men and Women Together*, (New York: Harper & Row, 1983), 48-64. They need to be read in the light of Rizutto, *The Birth of the Living God*, op. cit.

thesis of similarity between parental images and images of God 'that they give definite support to psychoanalytic notions regarding the impact of family relationships on religious feelings and ideas.'[30]

Freud's atheistic psychology, with its hermeneutic of suspicion, which may have had its roots in his antipathy towards his own inadequate father, has tended to undermine the legitimacy of religious belief. I suspect that many of those who have become unbelievers in Western countries accept the Freudian notion that God is a childish projection and that religion is an irrational form of collective neurosis. However, we have seen that Paul Vitz has suggested that, even on its own terms, Freud's critique of religion and spirituality is highly questionable. One practical implication of Vitz's thesis is the need to encourage consistent caring of their children by loving fathers and mothers, because it models what the faithful love of God the Father/Mother is like. Deprived of that kind of love, many children are in danger of rejecting God with all the sad consequences that such rejection entails.

As for those who have experienced defective caring from their earthly fathers a number of points are relevant. Firstly, they need male mentors who will offer them fatherly love in a dependable and encouraging way by showing credible love. This kind of relationship can help to challenge and overcome the hurting, angry and mistrustful attitudes and images that were formed in childhood. Secondly, people who had a bad relationship with their fathers need help in exploring their damaging emotional consequences either through the help of counsellors or psychotherapists. Then soaking prayer for inner healing could help to undo the hurts of the past. Thirdly, those who feel their fathers failed them, need to understand why this was so. Often the cause was weakness rather than malice. Then, one way or the other, they need to offer their fathers the unconditional forgiveness that God offers to them. Fourthly, people who find it hard to believe in a Father God can pray something like

---

30. *The Birth of the Living God*, op. cit., 5.

this: 'God if you exist, if you are truly a Father who loves me, reveal your presence and love to my hurting heart so that I may
believe in you.' I'm convinced that anyone who sincerely prays
in this way will eventually experience the presence and love of
God, because scripture promises in Deut 4:29: 'If from there
(wherever you are emotionally) you seek the Lord your God,
you will find him if you look for him with all your heart and
with all your soul.'

CHAPTER EIGHT

Neurotheology and Spiritual Intelligence

Many people are familiar with St Augustine's phrase, 'My heart is restless until it rests in you, my God.' This innate sense of religious yearning has been referred to by eminent Catholic theologian, Karl Rahner, as an obediential potency of the human person for supernatural grace.[1] Psychologist Carl Jung hypothesised that, from a psychological point of view, this capacity was rooted in the God archetype. Archetypes are like the wooden frameworks that builders first construct before filling them with concrete. In other words, the God archetype represents a capacity of the self rather than a content of the unconscious mind. It is open to the possibility of an experience of the divine. All people everywhere have this potential. Jung said: 'When I say as a psychologist that God is an archetype, I mean by that the 'type' in the psyche. The word 'type' is, as we know, derived from *typos*, 'blow' or 'imprint'; thus an archetype pre-supposes an imprinter ... The religious point of view, understandably enough, puts the accent on the imprinter, whereas scientific psychology emphasises the *typos*, the imprint – the only thing it can understand. The religious point of view understands the imprint as the working of an imprinter; the scientific point of view understands it as the symbol of an unknown and incomprehensible content.'[2] Jung suspected that this psychological archetype was anchored in some kind of biological capacity. In other words, God has endowed the body and mind with a natural capacity for Spirit given awareness of God. As the Catholic adage goes, 'grace

---

1. Cf. Rahner & Vorgrimler, 'Potentia Obedientalis', *Theological Dictionary*, (New York: Herder & Herder, 1968), 367.
2. 'Psychology and Alchemy,' *Collected Works* (1943) Vol 12, p 14.

builds on nature.' Some recent genetic and neurological research seems to lend support this point of view.

In the autumn of 2004, Dr Dean Hamer, a geneticist, suggested in a book entitled, *The God Gene: How Faith is Hardwired into Our Genes*,[3] that there is a gene, VMAT2 which facilitates religious experience. He asked 1000 people 226 questions in order to determine how spiritually connected they felt to the universe. The higher their score, the greater the person's capacity for self-forgetfulness, transpersonal identification and mysticism. Hammer proposed the hypothesis that this capacity was rooted in the activity of the, so called, God-gene. Those with VMAT2 have a freer-flowing vesicular monoamine transporter that regulates the flow of mood-altering chemicals in the brain, and as a result they are more likely to develop spiritual beliefs. He felt that this conclusion was supported by the fact that studies on twins showed that those with this gene were more likely to develop a spiritual belief. That would mean growing up in a religious environment had little effect on religious or spiritual convictions.

Speaking about great religious figures of the past, Hammer has said that because Buddha, Muhammad and Jesus all shared a series of mystical experiences or alterations in consciousness, it was highly likely that they carried the gene. This means that the tendency to be spiritual is part of genetic makeup; more the result of nature than nurture. Like intelligence it could skip a generation. Hammer goes on to explain that many other genes and environmental factors are also involved in being religious/spiritual. Nevertheless, the gene is important because it points to the mechanisms by which spirituality is manifested in the brain. He concludes by saying that religious believers can point to the existence of God genes as one more sign of the creator's ingenuity – a clever way to help humans acknowledge and embrace the divine presence. It is only fair to say that Hammer's work is new and controversial. Some theologians argue that this is yet another instance of reductionism, similar to Rene Descartes's belief that

---

3. (New York: Doubleday, 2004).

the pineal gland, a tiny protuberance deep in the brain, was *the* point of connection between body and spirit.

A God Spot in the Brain?
In recent years a number of books by d'Aquili, Newberg and Alper have engaged in what is known as neurotheology or less commonly, biotheology.[4] It is a search for the place(s) in the brain where religious beliefs originate. Investigations of this kind have attempted to show how some scientists, who study the brain, have discovered the part of the cortex that makes it possible to have spiritual experiences. A number of studies are particularly significant in this regard.

In the first, Michael Persinger, a Canadian neuro-psychologist, carried out original research in the 1990s. He fitted a hat-like magnetic stimulator on his own head. It beamed a rapidly fluctuating magnetic field at selected areas of his brain, specifically the temporal lobes, i.e. the areas of the brain just under our foreheads. As a result of the magnetic stimulation Persinger says that he 'saw God'. Subsequently, he found that he could induce all kinds of religious experiences, such as out-of-the-body and mystical experiences by stimulating appropriate parts of the brain.

The second scientist whose work is worth noting is Vilayanur Ramachandran, of San Diego University. In 1998 he published a book entitled, *Phantoms in the Brain*.[5] In it he maintained that, following seizures, about 25% of epileptics reported deeply moving spiritual experiences. They included a feeling of a divine presence and a sense of direct communication with God. Everything around them was imbued with cosmic significance. They said such things as, 'I finally understand what it is all about ... Suddenly it all makes sense ... I have insight into the

---

4. d' Aquili and Newberg, *The Mystical Mind: Probing The Biology of Mysticism*, (Minneapolis: Fortress Press, 1999); Newberg, *God Won't Go Away: How Faith is Hardwired into our Genes* (New York: Ballantine, 2001); Alper, *The God Part of the Brain: A Scientific Interpretation of Human Spirituality and God* (New York: Rogue Press, 2001)
5. (New York: Harper/Collins, 1998).

true nature of the universe.' In *The Idiot*, Fyodor Dostoyevsky has Prince Myshkin, an epileptic, say: 'I have really touched God. He came into me, myself; yes, God exists, I cried. You all, healthy people can't imagine the happiness which we epileptics feel during the second before our attack.' As a result of examining the epileptics who reported such significant religious experiences, Ramachandran and other researchers have suggested that there appears to be a 'God spot' in the front left temporal lobes of the brain. Briefly put, they suspect that epileptic seizures cause damage to some of the pathways which connect the area of the brain that deals with sensory information to the amygdala which gives such information emotional significance. As a result, these patients can perceive an unusual depth of spiritual meaning in every object and event. Jeffrey Saver and John Rabin of the University of California in Los Angeles Neurological Research Centre have suggested that the available documentary evidence indicates that a number of the world's spiritual leaders suffered from temporal lobe epilepsy. The list would include people such as the prophet Ezekiel, the apostle Paul, Mohammed and Joan of Arc. Not surprisingly, scientists like Persinger and Ramachandran have referred to the part of the brain that facilitates religious experience as the 'God Spot' or the 'God Module.'

A third area of research involved a study of the kinds of brain waves associated with different states of mind. In a wakened state, humans typically have a brain frequency of Beta rhythms, i.e. of about 13 cycles per second. When we meditate, our brains shift to Alpha rhythms of 8 to 12 cycles per second. When people experience a mystical sense of oneness with the world around them, their brains shift to Theta rhythms with even fewer cycles per second. Speaking about such oceanic experiences, Dr Eugene D'Aquili said that they result in the subject's attainment of a state of rapturous transcendence and absolute wholeness that conveys such overwhelming power and strength that the subject has the sense of experiencing absolute reality. This is the state of absolute unitary being (AUB). Indeed, so ineffable is this state that for those who experience it, even the memory of it carries a sense of greater reality than the reality of the everyday world. However, D'Aquili and Newberg felt that it was important to go beyond brain wave research to identify the nature and location of the changes that take place in the brain during mystical experiences.

It can be difficult to unobtrusively track the neuronal activity of people in intense states of meditation or prayer without jolting them back into everyday perception. However, using Single Photon Emission Computed Tomography, or (SPECT), scientists Newburg and D' Aquili were able to track neuronal activity in a small number of Tibetan Buddhists and Franciscan nuns without disturbing them. With an intravenous tube in their arm, each meditator focused intently on a single, usually religious, image until they achieved their familiar meditative sense of oneness. When each meditator felt this sense of union, he or she tugged on a string to alert the researchers, who then injected a radioactive tracer into the intravenous line. The tracer went to the regions of the brain where blood flow was highest. A computer scanner then made a snapshot showing the regions with the most circulation, which indicated where the greatest neuronal activity was taking place.

Since the meditators were focusing intently, the prefrontal cortex, associated with attention, lit up. But more strikingly, the parietal lobes showed very little activity. They are associated with the orientation of the body and processing information about time and space. More specifically, the left superior parietal lobe creates the perception of the physical body's boundaries. The right superior parietal lobe creates the perception of the physical space outside of the body. Blocked off from neuronal activity, the parietal lobes cannot create a sensation of boundary between the physical body and the outside world, which may explain the meditator's sense of oneness with the universe (AUB). Since the parietal lobes were also unable to perform their usual task of creating a linear perception of time, meditators achieved a sensation of infinity and timelessness. As David Wulff of Wheaton College, Massachusetts, points out, the current brain scanning studies, along with the consistency of spiritual experiences across cultures, history, and religions, suggest a common core that is likely a reflection of structures and processes in the human brain.

A fourth area of research involved twins. For instance, the Commonwealth University of Virginia studied 30,000 sets. The researchers concluded that: 'Although the transmission of religiousness has been assumed to be purely cultural, behaviour genetic studies have demonstrated that genetic factors play a role in the individual differences in some religious traits ... Religious affiliation is primarily a culturally transmitted phenomenon; religious attitudes and practices are moderately influenced by genetic factors.'[6] Another study of twins, conducted by the University of Minnesota, was more forthright about its conclusions: 'Studies of twins raised apart suggest that 5% of the extent of our religious interests and attitudes are determined by our genes.'[7] Taken together, these two studies do not seem to confirm Hammer's conclusions about the role of genetics in religion and spirituality. Taken together these different research projects suggest quite strongly that, besides the issue of nurture, there is a genetic and neurological explanation, albeit a small one, for people's predisposition in favour of spirituality and religion.

Does the Brain Create God?

What are we to make of all this? The role of the temporal lobes in the religious experience of epileptics, probably throws light on the way in which all of us can have such experiences. However, non-believers such as Professor Susan Greenfield – who, some time ago, presented a fascinating series about the brain on TV – maintain that awareness of God is merely the outcome of the complex activities of the temporal lobes of the brain. In other words, rather than being God's creation, the brain is the creator of God experiences. This is typical of the reductionist approach

6. *The God Part of the Brain*, op. cit., 133.
7. *The God Part of the Brain*, op. cit., 134.

of some scientists. It is worth noting, however, that when eminent neuroscientist, Andrew Newberg, was asked whether the
brain created the idea of God, or God created the brain, he responded: 'Neuroscience can't answer that question.' He is right
of course. Science can merely describe empirical phenomena, it
cannot make metaphysical judgements about them. To do so
would involve category error, where one jumps from empirical
description to metaphysical assertion. That said, those who espouse the validity of spiritual experience can quite justifiably
point to the fact that the brain is hard-wired for such awareness.

It should be noted that the controversial research referred to,
especially that of Dean Hammer, is still in its infancy. As many
scientists and religious leaders have pointed out, a lot still remains to be discovered about the interrelated subjects of the
God-gene and the God-spot in the brain. That said, rather than
being threatened by genuine scientific breakthroughs in these
areas of knowledge, believers can welcome them, not only for
their own sake, as advances in human understanding, but also
because they tend to lend support to the authenticity of their
religious claims. What contemporary scientific research is trying
to indicate, is the precise way in which our human nature is pre-
disposed, both genetically and neurologically, to have graced
spiritual experiences.

Forms of Intelligence
Current research seems to point to the fact that to be religious is
as second nature to being human as such things as music,
language, dance or sport. So, if you sometimes suspect that
contemporary science is pulling the rug from under your most
cherished religious convictions, be reassured; nowadays it increasingly tends to support them. At this point we will explore
an example of how this is happening in the study of human intelligence.

I.Q.
At the beginning of the twentieth century the notion of an

Intelligence Quotient (IQ) was introduced by French psychologist Alfred Binet (1857-1911). Some time later Lewis Terman (1877-1956) developed the original notion of an intelligence quotient. IQ tests were intended to measure serial thinking, i.e. how quickly and comprehensively a person could engage in insightful, abstract thinking. Terman proposed this scale for classifying IQ scores:

Over 140 – Genius or near genius

120-140 – Very superior intelligence

110-119 – Superior intelligence

90-109 – Normal or average intelligence

80-89 – Dullness

70-79 – Borderline deficiency

Under 70 – Definite feeble-mindedness

The properties of the normal distribution apply to IQ scores:

50% of IQ scores fall between 90 and 110

70% of IQ scores fall between 85 and 115

95% of IQ scores fall between 70 and 130

99.5% of IQ scores fall between 60 and 140

There is evidence which indicates that an established minimum IQ is necessary to succeed in different tasks. For example, while one might need an IQ of around 115 to 124 to get a basic degree one would need an IQ of 130 or more to get a PhD. A tiny percentage of the population would have exceptionally high intelligence, for example, William James Sidis (1898-1944) had the highest IQ ever recorded, an estimated 250-300. He could read at 18 months, taught himself Latin at 2, Greek at 3, had written a treatise on anatomy at 4. He passed the Massachusetts Institute of Technology's entrance exam at the age of eight and entered Harvard at 11. It is thought that in adult life, Sidis could speak 40 languages! Clearly, there is no necessary connection between IQ and spirituality. As Jesus said: 'I praise you, Father, Lord of heaven and earth, because you have hidden these things from the wise and learned, and revealed them to little children' (Mt 11:25).

In more recent years a psychologist called Howard Gardner

has suggested that the notion of I.Q. is too narrow. In an influential book, *Frames Mind: The Theory of Multiple Intelligence*,[8] he suggested that there are seven interrelated forms of intelligence. He added an eighth following the publication of the book.

1. *Linguistic* intelligence: a sensitivity to the meaning and order of words.

2. *Logical-mathematical* intelligence: ability in mathematics and other complex logical systems.

3. *Musical* intelligence: the ability to understand and create music. Musicians, composers and dancers show a heightened musical intelligence.

4. *Spatial* intelligence: the ability to 'think in pictures,' to perceive the visual world accurately, and recreate or alter it in the mind or on paper. Spatial intelligence is highly developed in artists, architects, designers and sculptors.

5. *Bodily-kinesthetic* intelligence: the ability to use one's body in a skilled way, for self-expression or towards a goal. Mime artists, dancers, sports men and women, and actors are among those who display bodily-kinesthetic intelligence.

6. *Interpersonal* intelligence: an ability to perceive and understand other individuals, their moods, desires, and motivations. Political and religious leaders, skilled parents, teachers, and therapists use this intelligence.

7. *Intrapersonal* intelligence: an understanding of one's own emotions. Some novelists and counsellors use their own self-awareness to help others.

8. *Naturalist* intelligence. It refers to the ability to recognise and classify plants, minerals, and animals, including rocks and grass and all variety of flora and fauna.

It is interesting to note that Gardner makes no mention of spirituality in his classification.

E.Q.

In 1996 Ronald Goleman published a book entitled, *Emotional*

---

8. (New York: Basic Books, 1983).

Intelligence.[9] In a way he combined Gardner's interpersonal and intrapersonal forms of intelligence. He suggested that those who are mature, self-aware and endowed with high levels of empathy are good at handling relationships and conflict situations. As a result one could say that they are intelligent in an affective rather than a purely cognitive sense. This aptitude is sometimes referred to as associative thinking. Goleman refers to this kind of savvy as EQ. Research has shown that this form of affective intelligence is based on the associative neural wiring of the brain. While emotional intelligence can, and often does play an important role in loving relationships, Goleman does not discuss the spiritual significance of emotional intelligence. However, as American theologian, Jonathan Edwards pointed out in his classic book, *The Religious Affections* (1746), 'For although to true religion there must indeed be something else besides affection (i.e. feelings), yet true religion consists so much in the affections that there can be no true religion without them.'[10]

S.Q.

More recently, Danah Zohar and her husband Ian Marshall, have suggested in their book *Spiritual Intelligence: The Ultimate Intelligence,*[11] that, neither IQ or EQ separately or in combination is sufficient to explain the full complexity of human intelligence. They point to the obvious fact that people also have altruistic spiritual capacities for unitive thinking, which are made possible by the God Gene and the God spot in the brain. They advert to the fact that there are discernibly different brain waves associated with spiritual as opposed to other kinds of experience. They describe spiritual understanding as 'soul intelligence' that seeks, in the words of T. S. Eliot 'a further union, a deeper communion.'[12]

Zohar & Marshall say that spiritual intelligence is the intelligence with which we access our deepest meanings, values, pur-

---

10. (Edinburgh: Banner of Truth, 1984), 49.
11. (London: Bloomsbury, 2000)
12. *Four Quartets* (London: Faber & Faber, 1969), East Coker, l, 200.

poses, and higher motivations. It is the intelligence with which we address and solve problems, the intelligence with which we can place our actions and our lives in a wider, richer, meaning-giving context, the intelligence with which we can work out that one course of action is more meaningful than another. Spiritual intelligence enables people to experience a simultaneous sense of belonging to the universe, other people, their deepest selves and God. In the light of this sense of connection with mystery, in and through their everyday relationships, they seem to have an intuitive sense of how spiritual awareness should impinge on decision making.

Zohar and Marshall say that SQ 'rests in that deep part of the self that is connected to wisdom from beyond the ego, or conscious mind; it is the intelligence with which we not only recognise existing values, but with which we creatively discover new values.'[13] Instead of being orientated towards survival, this higher capacity, or SQ, adds to the quality of life. Zohar and Marshall say that indications of a highly developed SQ would be:

- The capacity to be flexible, i.e. actively and spontaneously adaptive
- A high degree of self awareness
- A capacity to face and use suffering
- A capacity to face and transcend pain
- The quality of being inspired by vision and values
- A reluctance to cause unnecessary harm
- A tendency to see the connections between diverse things, i.e. being holistic
- A marked tendency to ask why? and what if? and to seek fundamental answers
- Having a capacity to work against convention
- Perhaps a servant leader, someone who is responsible for bringing higher vision and value to others and showing them how to use it.[14]

13. *Spiritual Intelligence*, op. cit., 9
14. *Spiritual Intelligence*, op. cit., 15-16.

It could be said in passing that these qualities are quite similar to the ones associated with self-actualisers in Maslow's psychology. Zohar and Marshall reflect a common, not to say fashionable, distinction when they maintain that spiritual intelligence has no necessary connection with religion or any other organised belief system. Of course SQ may find expression through institutional religion, but being religious doesn't necessarily indicate that the person has a high SQ. On the other hand, in spite of having no religious affiliation, many agnostics and atheists do have a high SQ.

The Bible esteems wisdom, or spiritual intelligence, very highly. In 1 Kgs 3:7-12 and 2 Chron 1:2-14, we are told how Solomon went to a shrine at Gibeon, four miles northwest of Jerusalem. There he had a religious dream in which God said to him. 'Ask what I should give you.' The king replied, 'Give your servant an understanding mind to govern your people, able to discern between good and evil.' The Lord was so pleased by Solomon's single minded desire for spiritual intelligence that he promised him: 'Because you have not asked for yourself long life or riches, or for the life of your enemies, but have asked for yourself understanding to discern what is right, I now do according to your word. Indeed I give you a wise and discerning mind.' In 1 Kgs 4:29-30 we are told that: 'God gave Solomon very great wisdom, discernment and breadth of understanding as vast as the sand on the seashore.'

When the Bible speaks of wisdom, such as Solomon's, it refers principally to a spirit of discernment, which is the fruit of a mature, intimate relationship with God. As Heb 5:14 says: 'Solid food is for the mature, for those who have their faculties trained by practice to distinguish good from evil.' The wisdom of Solomon was so great that we are told how the queen of Sheba,[15] came a long distance to visit him. 'Solomon answered all her questions; there was nothing hidden from Solomon that he could not explain to her' (1 Kgs 10:3). It is interesting to note

---

15. Sheba may mean seven, a highly symbolic number. Cf *Dictionary of Symbols*, (London: Penguin, 1996), 861-862.

that Jesus referred to Sheba's visit: 'She came from the ends of the earth to listen to the wisdom of Solomon, and see, something greater than Solomon is here!' (Mt 12:42). As Paul was later to testify: 'Christ is the wisdom of God' (1 Cor 1:24).

We all need the gift of wisdom (cf Is 11:2), the kind of spiritual intelligence which enables us, like Jesus, to discern, amid the illusions and false inspirations of everyday life, which decisions and actions are inspired by the Spirit of God and which are not. As the author of Col 1:9-10 testified: 'We have not ceased praying for you and asking that you may be filled with that knowledge of God's will in all spiritual wisdom and understanding, so that you may lead lives worthy of the Lord, fully pleasing to him.'

Not surprisingly, the gifts of wisdom and understanding were much appreciated by St Thomas Aquinas, who not only had a high IQ, he also was blessed with a remarkably high SQ as well. Speaking of inspired understanding, St Thomas wrote: 'It enables us to discern rightly and surely what to believe and what not to believe. Man's knowledge comes by reasoning and proof, but God's by simple insight, and the Holy Spirit's gift is a shared likeness in God's knowledge.'[16] He described inspired wisdom in these words: 'It knows by a kind of unity with divine things, the actual things in which we believe, and so corresponds to the virtue which unites us to God, namely charity.'[17]

St Thomas also spoke about practical wisdom, which he referred to as connatural knowledge. He maintained that loving people who are united to God have a quasi instinctive ability to discern, in the circumstances of everyday life, between good and evil, what is appropriate and inappropriate. Thomist scholar Garrigou Legrange has written by way of explanation, 'As a bee or carrier pigeon is directed by instinct, and acts with a wonderful certainty, revealing the Transcendent Intelligence which directs them, just so, says St Thomas, the spiritual person is inclined to act, not principally through the movement of his own

---

16. *Summa Theologiae: A Concise Translation*, ed. Timothy Mc Dermott, (London: Methuen, 1991), 338.
17. *Summa Theologiae: A Concise Translation*, op. cit., 339.

will, but by the instinct of the Holy Spirit.'[18] Pope John Paul II referred to this form of spiritual intelligence when he wrote: 'It is the "heart" converted to the Lord and to the love of what is good which is really the source of true judgements of conscience. Indeed, in order to "prove what is the will of God, what is good and acceptable and perfect" [a]Rom 12:2), knowledge of God's law in general is certainly necessary, but it is not sufficient: what is essential is a sort of "connaturality" between man and the true good.'[19]

Conclusion

While it would be true to say that neurotheology is in its infancy, it has made an interesting contribution to the debate about the relationship between spirituality and science. On the plus side, it indicates that from an anthropological point of view we have a God-given, biological and psychological capacity for spirituality. As such it is helping to reconcile science and religion. Zohar and Marshall believe that of the three forms of intelligence, cognitive, emotional and spiritual, the latter is not only the most important, it can integrate and fulfil the potential in the other two. On the minus side, there are at least two obvious dangers. Firstly, while neurotheology focuses on mystical experiences of oneness, what d'Aquili referred to as a sense of absolute unitary being (AUB), these are not typical of what people normally experience in the course of their everyday spiritual lives. Secondly, this new branch of research can be reductionist and excessively materialistic. As a result it can dismiss religious experience, as conscious relationship with the mystery of God, as nothing but the product of electro-chemical events in the brain.

18. *Christian Perfection and Contemplation* (St Louis: Herder, 1946), 271.
19. *Veritatis Splendor* (1993), par 64.

CHAPTER NINE

A Psycho-Spiritual Study of Vincent de Paul[1]

Psycho-biographies are a relatively new genre of literature. They have become increasingly popular since the end of World War II. There are many of them, such as Erik Erickson's *Ghandi's Truth*,[2] William Meissner's *Ignatius of Loyola: The Psychology of a Saint*,[3] Robert Waldron's, *Thomas Merton in Search of his Soul: A Jungian Perspective*[4] and John Welch's *Spiritual Pilgrims: Carl Jung and Teresa of Avila*.[5] To a considerable extent, the success of books like these depends on the accuracy of the available bio-graphical material and the validity of the psychological theories used to interpret it. The legitimacy of examining Vincent de Paul's early adulthood, from a psychological point of view, is justified by the fact that, as St Thomas Aquinas pointed out, 'grace presupposes nature.'[6] To examine the dynamics of Vincent's natural growth is to study the anthropology of the Spirit.

This brief and tentative study will examine a period of St Vincent de Paul's life from his ordination at the age of nineteen in 1600 to the time he vowed to serve the poor in 1614. For the sake of clarity we will divide these 14 years into three separate stages.

- 1600-1605 early-adult transition, when he got his degree in theology.
- 1605-1608 a time of crisis when Vincent went missing.
- 1608-1614 years of purification and transformation.

1. Published in *Colloque* (Winter 2005), 91-106.
2. (New Haven, CT : Yale University Press, 1992)
3. (New York: Norton, 1969)
4. (Notre Dame: Ave Maria Press, 1994)
5. (New York: Paulist Press, 1982)
6. *Summa Theologiae: A Concise Translation*, ed. Timothy Mc Dermott, (London: Methuen, 1991), 296.

These reflections will focus mainly on the significance of Vincent's missing years, when he claimed to have been a captive in North Africa.

We will use three complementary kinds of information. Firstly, there are the known historical facts: biographical details in letters, conferences and Louis Abbely's three volume *The Life of the Venerable Servant of God, Vincent de Paul* (1664).[7] That said, we know relatively little about his early days. For example, Pierre Coste devotes only fifty pages of his 1500 page biography to the first third of Vincent's life. As two of my learned colleagues have pointed out, the paucity of biographical detail inevitably weakens the thesis put forward in this chapter. Secondly, we will attempt to interpret the available facts in the light of contemporary psychology, especially of the developmental and Jungian kinds. Thirdly, we will use the Ignatian notion of two distinct stages in spiritual maturation, one self-centred, the other God-centred, to interpret Vincent's experience. By utilising these varied resources we can hope to gain some insight into the psycho-spiritual dynamics of Vincent's inner life during the formative years of his early adulthood. Not only was his future sanctity rooted in this period, it also marked the time when his experience of the Christian life was most like our own. It is my hope that, as we become aware of the process of Vincent's early growth in human and Christian maturity, we ourselves will be enabled to 'become mature, attaining to the whole measure of the fullness of Christ' (Eph 4:13).

1. Early-adult transition 1600-1605

In his *Seasons of a Man's* Life Daniel Levinson says that men can expect to enter an early-adult transition between the ages of 17 and 22.[8] This is a bridging period between adolescence and early adulthood. The main pre-occupations at this time are a desire to get established in the world and to begin working out an adult sense of identity. These issues tend to be highlighted in what he

7. (New York: New City Press, 1993)
8. (New York: Ballantine, 1979), 20, 56.

calls 'marker events'. Vincent reached one such milestone when he was ordained. Having become a deacon at the tender age of 17, Vincent had applied to the Bishop of Dax for permission to be ordained a priest. It would appear that the teaching of the recent Council of Trent (1545), which stipulated that a man was not eligible for ordination until he was 24, had not yet been fully implemented in France. Vincent may have lied about his age to get his dimissorial letter. Then he was ordained by a saintly old bishop, François de Bourdeilles, who was to die one month later. The future reformer of the clergy got off to a rather shaky start himself by means of an irregular, though not an invalid, ordination.[9] No wonder his confrères were never to know anything about its date, place, or circumstances. Prudence, rather than modesty, may have been the motive.

Vincent found it hard to get established in his priestly role. The Bishop of Dax offered him a parish but there were legal problems, so he continued to live as he had before. He ran a small school, continued to study at the university and visited Rome. It was a time when he seemed to rely mainly on his own considerable talents for success. He got his bachelor's degree in theology in 1604, which entitled him to comment, before university students, on the second book of Peter Lombard's *Sentences*. However, he was beset by financial difficulties. He had borrowed money to set up his school. As he admitted, he had a 'need for money to take care of debts I had incurred.'[10]

We don't know what the priesthood meant to him. There is no indication that he had a personal vocation as a boy. As a talented, devout member of a large family, his parents urged him to become a priest, much in the same way as a suitable marriage might be arranged. They hoped that, besides doing his pastoral work, he would be able to help them financially. While Vincent seemed content to go along with their wishes, there is no clear

---

9. On the subject of the ordination see Jose Maria Roman, 'The Priestly Journey of St Vincent de Paul: The Beginnings 1600-1612' *Vincentiana* (May-June, 2000), 209.

10. Pujo, *Vincent de Paul: The Trailblazer* (Notre Dame University Press, 2003), 21.

indication that he had fully embraced the priesthood in an interior way. As a dedicated young Catholic he was committed to the role of priesthood in an extrinsic rather than an intrinsic way. As was noted earlier in chapter three, Gordon Allport, proposed such a distinction in his *The Individual and His Religion* when he maintained that there were two forms of religion, an immature and a mature variety.[11] At this point in his life it would appear that Vincent was more motivated by what God would do for him than by what he could do for God. Fifty years later he seemed to admit as much, when he wrote: 'As for me, if I had known what it was all about when I was rash enough to enter it, as I have come to know since, I would rather have worked the soil than engage in such a fearsome state of life.'[12] Two incidents in 1605 seem to confirm the fact that Vincent's religion tended to be immature and extrinsic in the period just after his ordination.

Early in the year 1605, Vincent de Paul headed off to Bordeaux on a secret mission. He said it would be rash to mention what it was about. He did acknowledge that he was 'on the track of a project my foolhardiness forbids me to mention.' It is possible that he had the hope of being offered a good abbey or a rich parish. 'What we do know for certain – on Vincent's own admission – is that the business promised to be of great advantage to him, and that it would involve considerable expenditure.'[13] But it all came to nothing, and Vincent returned home with an empty purse as a result of the travel expenses incurred.

When he got back from the South, Vincent was much relieved to find that he had been left some tracts of land and furniture in a woman's will. However, there was a complication. The only way he could get his hands on the 300-400 ecus his property was worth, was to extract the sum from a man in Marseilles who had defrauded the old lady. To finance his trip and prospective legal action, Vincent had to borrow money. He hired a horse and

11. (New York: Macmillan, 1971), 31-112.
12. Letter from Vincent de Paul to Canon Saint-Martin (S.V 5:567)
13. P. Coste, *The Life and Works o f St Vincent de Paul*, vol 1 (New York: New City Press, 1987), 26.

set off. The future apostle of charity showed little compassion when he tracked down the man he called 'a scamp'. He had him thrown into jail until he would agree to pay the debt. This he did in due course. This was a far cry from the text 'be mindful of prisoners as if you were sharing their imprisonment' (Heb 13:3). Meantime Vincent sold the hired horse. It was a bit like selling a rented car to raise money. As Bernard Pujo observes: 'With this transaction, he made himself guilty of a crime which, in those days, was severely punished with imprisonment or even forced labour on the galleys.'[14]

In 1605 Vincent was undoubtedly a talented, well qualified, and well intentioned young priest of 25. But he had his faults. He could act in an unscrupulous, callous way if it served his desire for ecclesiastical and financial advancement. In fact he was the kind of troublesome priest that a present-day bishop or provincial would probably ask to see for 'a wee chat'! Clearly he wasn't saintly at this point in his life.

2. The missing years, 1605-1608
Levinson says that early-adulthood begins about 22 and ends when a man is 45 or so. During that time he can expect to experience more marker events: periods of transition that will challenge his values and sense of self. For Vincent one of these crises took place between the ages of 24 and 27 when he decided to return from Marseilles to Narbonne by sea. We are not absolutely sure where he ended up. In letters, written in 1608, to his mentor Monsieur De Comet, he said that he had been a prisoner in Tunis, having been captured by Turkish brigantines during a sea voyage. While it is certain that Vincent wrote the letters, doubt has been cast on their veracity.

Stafford Poole suggests that there are three possibilities.[15] Firstly, the letters are completely true. However, a scholar named Grandchamps has shown that this option is not viable

---

14. *Vincent de Paul: The Trailblazer*, op. cit., 25
15. *Tunisian Captivity: A survey of the controversy* (St John's Seminary, California), 71.

from the historical point of view. Secondly, the letters could be dismissed as completely false. Thirdly, parts of the letters could be accepted as true, other parts rejected as false. After weighing all the evidence, Poole concludes that the letters are probably false. This would explain why Vincent never mentioned his captivity. Both Brother Ducournau and Louis Abelly testify to his life-long silence about it. It would also explain why Vincent made such frantic efforts to have the letters destroyed when they were discovered some 50 years after their composition. At the age of 79 he wrote these words to Canon de Saint-Martin: 'I entreat you by all the favours that God has been pleased to give you, to do me the favour of sending me that wretched letter that makes mention of Turkey. I speak of the one that was discovered among the papers of the late Monsieur De Comet. I beg you again by the heart of Jesus Christ Our Lord to do me this favour that I ask you, as quickly as possible.'[16] Was Vincent's silence about his captivity and his desire to have the letters destroyed, motivated by the same kind of embarrassment he felt about his ordination?

If Vincent wasn't in North Africa where was he? There are a number of possibilities. Jean Calvet says, rather gratuitously, that Vincent may have been in Provence where 'he was leading a dissipated life on the money obtained from the debtor and the proceeds of the horse.'[17] When he came to his senses, he surfaced again. Calvet believed that the account of Vincent's captivity in North Africa was merely a tall tale that he told Monsieur de Comet and his family. Marcel Emerit has suggested that Vincent disappeared because he had been condemned to the galleys for the theft of the hired horse. Having rowed for two years, he was supposed to have escaped and taken refuge in Avignon, a papal enclave.[18]

While some scholars are of the opinion that Vincent was never a captive in North Africa, others say that there isn't suffi-

---

16. Coste, op. cit., 40.
17. *St Vincent de Paul*, op. cit., 31.
18. Pujo, *St Vincent de Paul: The Trailblazer*, op. cit., 269.

cient reason to think that he lied about the missing years. Having weighed all the pros and cons, the late José Maria Roman concluded: 'As long as we have no proof that Vincent was in some other part of France, or in some foreign place, between 1605 and 1607, we have to accept his statement that he was a captive in Tunis at that time.'[19] Some years after publishing his authoritative biography of Vincent, Roman wrote an interesting article entitled, 'The Priestly Journey of St Vincent de Paul: The Beginnings 1600-1612'. It refers to recent studies by Pierre Miquel, Bernard Pujo and Bernard Koch CM which support the substantial truthfulness of the letters.[20] Wherever he was, I believe that Vincent endured a transitional crisis.

Jungian Archetypes
Having looked at the missing years from a strictly historical point of view we switch, now, to the perspective of personal narrative, where we look at the available data from a more psychological perspective. It could be argued that Vincent's letters constituted what is known as a root metaphor. Webster's *Third New International Dictionary* defines a root metaphor 'as a fundamental perspective or viewpoint based on a supposition of similarity of form between mental concepts and external objects which though not factually supportable determines the manner in which an individual structures his knowledge.' Vincent's account of his captivity is an obvious example of a root metaphor. He used the experience of his captivity in an alien land, whether true or fictional, as an analogy for his quest not only for individuation in a Jungian sense, but also for a personal, as opposed to a formal, sense of priestly identity. This personal myth enabled him to articulate the religious meanings that surfaced in his life at that time. Like a number of other writers, James and Evelyn Whitehead have suggested that there are three phases in the experience of psycho-spiritual passage.

---

19. *St Vincent de Paul: A Biography* (London: Melisende, 1999), 83.
20. *Vincentiana*, (May-June, 2000), 214.

1. *Onset and restlessness.* A time when our usual accommodation with life is disrupted. Old securities are challenged. There is a feeling of having been hi-jacked, of being a hapless and relatively helpless victim in a sort of no-man's-land. This is what happened when Vincent disappeared from society.
2. *Darkness and exploration.* A time of increased vulnerability, questioning and doubt. As illusions are challenged, the person begins to ask basic questions about his or her identity and values. As defence mechanisms break down, *chronos,* i.e. unredeemed, sequential time, becomes *kairos,* i.e. redeemed sacred time, as God begins to reveal the divine Self in a way that invites the person to change his or her values and sense of identity. This is what Vincent seems to have experienced during the missing years.
3. *Resolution and re-stabalisation.* As a person lets go of old ways of perception, s/he enters into a new stage of maturity and stability. This would be the symbolic implication of Vincent's re-emergence in French society.[21]

Some time ago it occurred to me that Vincent's captivity letters, whether fact or fiction, seemed to reveal a great deal about his unconscious state of mind. The story he told Monsieur de Comet had an archetypal quality. I wondered whether the events it described could be interpreted in a Jungian way as a symbol of the hero's journey into the underworld where he has to do battle with all kinds of powerful foes, only to re-emerge, endowed with new strength and wisdom. As one Jungian reference book observes: 'The hero is a transitional being. His most human form is the priest … he represents the will and capacity to seek and undergo repeated transformations.'[22] I think that Vincent's account can be understood as a metaphor for a personal inner journey. So I'd like to propose a tentative interpretation.

Unlike Freud, Jung believed that besides the personal uncon-

21. Cf Pat Collins, 'The Pain of Self-discovery', *Intimacy and the Hungers of the Heart* (Dublin: Columba, 1991), 58-73.
22. Samuels, Shorter & Plaut, 'The Hero', *A Critical Dictionary of Jungian Analysis,* (London: Routledge & Keegan Paul, 1986), 66.

scious, where our personal memories and their associated feelings are stored, there is also the collective unconscious. According to Jung, it includes the collective memory of the human race. Its dynamics are structured by archetypes, which have developed over the centuries. As was mentioned in a previous chapter, they are psychic capacities whose potential can be consciously activated by feeling laden symbols in myths, dreams and fairy tales. Archetypes are psychological equivalents of our biological instincts, which have such a profound effect upon the way we experience the world. There are four of them: the *persona, animus/anima*, shadow and the self.

1.   *The persona.* This is the self we present to the world, the one that we think will be accepted, approved and liked. It is the packaging of the ego, it's mask, it's uniform. As such it is the social self, the one that conforms to the expectations associated with one's role. Because we have many roles we can have many sides to our personas. There is always a danger that one's persona takes over to such a point that a person identifies entirely with it.

2.   *The animus/anima.* The word sex in English comes from the Latin *secare* which means 'to cut', i.e. 'to divide'. The sexes are divided in two inter-related ways. Firstly, men and women are divided from one another by physical and psychological differences. Some of the latter are due to nature, others to nurture , i.e. the influences of our cultural prejudices and stereotypes. Secondly, men and women are divided within themselves. Carl Jung has suggested that all of us are bi-sexual from a psychological point of view. As a man I am consciously, and predominantly male. But at an unconscious level there is a feminine dimension or *anima*, as Jung called it. Conversely, while women are predominantly and consciously female, at an unconscious level there is a masculine dimension or *animus* to use Jung's terminology.[23] It is mainly by

23. Cf John Sanford, *The Invisible Partners: How the Male and Female in each of Us Affects Our Relationships* (New York: Paulist Press, 1980); Some feminists argue that Jung is incorrect about the female *anima*. Cf Naomi Goldenberg, 'A Feminist Critique of Jung', *Women's Spirituality:*

means of heterosexual intimacy that men and women are reconciled to one another in love and experience an inner reconciliation of the male/female side of their natures. Jung believed that repression of the *animus* is very common in Western culture. In practical terms it means that many people tend rely on a left-brained, typically masculine approach to reality, one that stresses the importance of detached, objective reason and is epitomised by empirical science. What is often neglected and undervalued is a right-brained, typically feminine approach; one that stresses the importance of relationships, intuition and feeling, and is epitomised by religion and the arts. Christian wholeness is only possible when the man is aware of his *anima* because the soul is feminine in relation to God the Father and Jesus his Son.

3. *The Shadow*. Jung called the rejected, unaccepted side of the personality the shadow self. He wrote: 'Unfortunately there can be no doubt that man is, on the whole, less good than he imagines himself or wants to be. Everyone carries a shadow. The less it is embodied in the individual's conscious life, the blacker and denser it is.' In 1945 Jung gave his most succinct description of what the shadow involved when he said that, 'it is the thing a person has no wish to be.'[24] Robert Louis Stephenson's story of Dr Jekyll and Mr Hyde epitomises this polarity in the personality.[25] Whenever the darker side of our personality with its primitive urges threatens our ego ideal based, as it is, on idealistic beliefs and values, we reject it. It is buried alive in the unconscious. From there it can poison consciousness with negative feelings and attitudes. These we tend to project on to other people, seeing and disliking in them what we fail to see or to accept in ourselves. Incidentally the shadow often appears in dreams in the guise of an inferior

---

Resources for Christian Development, ed. Joann Wolski Conn (New York: Paulist Press, 1986), 150-158.

24. *Collected Works*, vol. 16, par. 470.

25. Cf John Sanford, *Evil: The Shadow Side of Reality* (New York: Crossroad, 1981).

individual, e.g. a beggar, or an inept person, who is the same gender as the dreamer.

4. *The self*. This is the central archetype which unites the personality, giving it a sense of oneness and firmness. In Jungian psychology the self encompasses the whole personality including the ego. 'The self is not only the centre,' Jung writes, 'but also the whole circumference which embraces both the conscious and unconscious; it is the centre of this totality, just as the ego is the centre of the conscious mind.'[26] Jung believed that the ego should not only be attentive to the external world, it should also be open to the inner whisperings of the self. In this connection feeling laden images, myths and dreams can be important. They enable a person to become sensitive to the personal and collective unconscious.

It would also be true to say that in Jungian psychology, the self is virtually synonymous with God because, at its core, it contains a God archetype which can only be filled and satisfied by means of religious experience of a numinous kind. For Christians, Christ is the supreme symbol of the self. Jung wrote: 'In the world of Christian ideas, Christ undoubtedly represents the self. As the apotheosis of individuality, the self has the attributes of uniqueness and of occurring once only in time.'[27] The self archetype is the one which orientates, directs and enables the development of the psyche and its other archetypes, so that the person increasingly achieves the goal of individuation, i.e. becoming whole through experiential contact with the numinous. If the self is unable to experience the divine, the personality becomes confused and neurotic.[28]

A Jungian Interpretation of the Missing Years
Using the Jungian hermeneutic, we can try to understand

---

26. *A Critical Dictionary of Jungian Analysis*, op. cit., 135
27. 'Christ as a Symbol of the Self' quoted by June Singer, *Boundaries of the Soul: The Practice of Jung's Psychology*, (New York: Anchor Doubleday, 1994), 393.
28. Cf C. Jung, 'Psychotherapists or Clergy', *Psychology and Western Religion* (London: Ark, 1988), 202.

Vincent's root metaphor. We begin with his sea journey. In the Bible there are a number of marvellous accounts of eventful sea voyages, such as Jonah's vicissitudes on the way to Niniveh, Jonah 1:4-15; the tempest described in Ps 107:23-30; the storm on the sea of Galilee in Mt 8:23-27; and St Paul's scary trip from a seaport in Asia Minor, to Rome. It is described in Acts 27. While these voyages can be understood in strictly historical terms, they can also be interpreted as metaphors. For example, the boat can be seen as the conscious ego which is buffeted by threatening wind and waves of emotion that emanate from the unconscious self. However, the person learns to cope by relying solely on the Lord. As Ps 89:8-9 puts it: 'O Lord God Almighty ... You rule over the surging sea; when its waves mount up, you still them.'

Vincent's tranquil voyage was suddenly and unexpectedly disrupted by his violent capture. He literally became the unwitting victim of 'the slings and arrows of outrageous fortune' when he was wounded during an attack upon his ship. Soon afterwards he had to endure the humiliation and hardship of captivity in a foreign land. These events were outward symbols of the onset of a traumatic inner crisis. It would involve a movement from self-determination to dependency, strength to weakness, from a sense of belonging to alienation. Paradoxically this dynamic represented Vincent's inner journey from an immature identification with his extroverted ego and its different roles, to a more introverted awareness of his spiritual self and his need to depend absolutely upon God. Arguably, divine providence had allowed his sufferings for a purpose. 'The Lord has led you ... in the wilderness, in order to humble you, testing you to know what is in your heart ... he humbled you by letting you experience hunger' (Deut 8:2-3).

The Fisherman

Vincent's captivity was punctuated by the fact that at different times he was the property of four slave owners. Each one of them seems to have symbolised some aspect of his inner conflicts. His first owner was a fisherman who wanted his help in catching fish. In the case of a priest this role would have had a strong symbolic resonance. In the gospel we read: 'Come, follow me,' Jesus said, 'and I will make you fishers of men' (Mk 1:17). But Vincent wrote: 'I was sold to a fisherman, but I have always been a very bad sailor; he was obliged to get rid of me.'[29] In other words, he didn't seem to have the stomach for the demands of priestly mission.

The Alchemist

Vincent's second owner was a learned and amiable alchemist. This is fascinating from a symbolic point of view. Carl Jung wrote a number of books on the psychological implications of alchemy.[30] I'd like to draw attention to points mentioned by Vincent, while suggesting a symbolic interpretation. He refers to the practice of trying to turn base metal into gold and mercury into silver, by human effort. Surely this is symbolic of a Faustian desire to be like God. It is also implicit in the reference to the philosopher's stone. As one author had written, 'If the Alchemist could impregnate the Stone with his own life, then he had discovered the secret of the Creator.' It would seem that Vincent was becoming aware of the fact that he had a Promethean tendency to depend more on his own human efforts, than on God. But to his credit, when the alchemist promised him riches and occult knowledge, if only he would convert to Islam, Vincent resisted this temptation against faith.[31] He also referred to the alchemist's talking skull. By means of ventriloquism he made it appear that he was receiving oracles from Allah. Symbolically, this may indicate that, at an unconscious level of awareness, Vincent saw himself as a false prophet, a priest who had only pretended to speak God's word. His account also refers to the

29. Jean Calvet, St Vincent de Paul (London: Burns Oates, 1952) , 24.
30. Cf Psychology and Alchemy; Alchemical Studies; Mysterium Coiunctionis.
31. In 'The Priestly Journey of St Vincent de Paul: The beginnings 1600-1612', op. cit., 215, Jose Mara Roman, indicates that many other captive priests in North Africa, engaged in scandalous dissentions and licentious behaviour, while failing to strengthen the faith of other Christian slaves.

fact that he had assisted the alchemist 'by keeping the fire going in ten or twelve furnaces.' Normally, fire is a symbol of strong emotion and passion. For instance, in 2 Tim 1:6 St Paul urged Timothy, a fellow presbyter, 'to fan into flame the gift of God, which is in you through the laying on of my hands' (i.e. in ordination). By his reference to the fire, did Vincent, inadvertently, reveal a desire for an inner ratification and renewal of his vocation to the priesthood?

The Heathen Farmer

When the alchemist was summoned to work for the supreme Sultan he gave Vincent to a third owner, his nephew, who Vincent described as 'an absolute heathen'. This seems to be a reference to his own shadow self, i.e. that part of himself which was the very antithesis of what a good priest should be. Jung believed that the extent that a person failed to recognise or accept his or her inferior self, was the extent to which s/he would be inclined to project it on to others. It looks as if the farmer, who owned him, was the carrier of some aspects of Vincent's shadow. However, when this man heard that the French king had dispatched an ambassador to Tunis with letters permitting him to reclaim Christian slaves, he dashed Vincent's hopes of freedom by selling him on to a renegade from Nice in Savoy.

The Renegade Christian

Vincent referred to his fourth owner as his 'natural enemy,' presumably because he had renounced his Christian faith and married three wives. Once again there is reason to think that this man too represented his alter-ego, and as such was also a carrier of Vincent's shadow. Inwardly, Vincent was split between his acceptable, idealistic priestly self and his unacknowledged heathen self, i.e. his instinctual urges unfettered by Christian ethics or beliefs. Jung once wrote: 'What drives people to war with themselves is the suspicion or the knowledge that they consist of two persons in opposition to one another.'[32] On another occa-

---

32. 'Psychotherapists or the Clergy', op. cit., 209.

sion he said: 'That I love my enemy is undoubtedly a great virtue … but what if I should discover … that I myself stand in need of the alms of my own kindness, that I myself am the enemy who must be loved – what then?'[33] He saw and despised in his master's infidelity what he failed to recognise or accept in himself.

The women in the story are also very interesting. There were the renegade's three wives, one Greek Orthodox and two Moslems. From a Jungian point of view they seem to be projections of different aspects of the *anima*, i.e. the repressed, feminine aspects of Vincent's unconscious mind. They are reminiscent of the three graces in classical mythology.[34] The Greek could have epitomised wisdom. She liked Vincent and treated him with kindness. But it was one of the non-Christian women who, surprisingly, had the greatest influence on Vincent. Having heard him talk about Christianity, it was she who urged her husband to return to the practice of his religion. It has always struck me that it was unlikely that the Moslem wife would have suggested – in such a self-sacrificing, benevolent way – that her husband should leave her in order to return to his homeland and the practice of his faith. Presumably, she, and any children she had, would have had been left with no means of economic support. Furthermore, the other two wives would have been furious. From a Jungian point of view, however, it would make sense to interpret this vignette as a reference to the way in which Vincent's unconscious mind urged him to sacrifice the many joys of marriage, symbolised by, not one, but three wives, in order to willingly embrace the charism of celibacy for the sake of the kingdom.

From a Jungian point of view, the benevolent power of Vincent's *anima*, was personified by the two sympathetic wives. Psychologists, who have written about the *anima*, say that this archetype can be either negative or positive. Vincent's experience, as symbolised by the Moslem wife, in particular, was en-

33. 'Psychotherapists or the Clergy', op. cit., 207.
34. T. Chetwynd, *A Dictionary of Symbols* (London: Paladin, 1982), 7.

tirely positive. Erich Neumann's study of the feminine archetype maintained that it had two possible characteristics, the ele-
mentary, i.e. to do with birth, nourishment, and caring; and the
transforming, i.e. to do with change and action.[35] Vincent had
the latter kind of experience. It is significant that he ultimately
attributed his deliverance to another woman, in the person of
Our Lady. For many Catholics she is the supreme symbol of the
benevolent aspects of the *anima*. Vincent testified: 'God always
enkindled in me a belief in deliverance, through the ceaseless
prayers I raised to him and the Holy Virgin Mary, by whose sole
intercession I firmly believe I was rescued.'[36]

Not only was Vincent influenced by the benign feminine archetype, so was his owner, who symbolically, was Vincent's
alter-ego. Some time later, they both made good their escape to
Europe. Symbolically, it sounds as if, inwardly, the dividing
wall of division between Vincent's acceptable priestly self and
his unacceptable, secular self had been breached in such a way
that inner alienation began to give way to a new form of integration (cf Eph 2:14). The crossing of the Mediterranean was reminiscent of the people of Israel crossing from slavery in Egypt, via
the Reed Sea, to the freedom of the promised land.

Individuation
There is reason to believe that during the missing years, Vincent
had got in touch with unconscious archetypes in such a way that
he was enabled to make an inward exodus from his selfish, controlling ego, to a more God-centred sense of priestly identity. In
Jungian terms his spiritual pilgrimage had enabled him to grow
in individuation. Over the years Jung offered numerous definitions of this complex concept. Having stated that individuation
played no small role in his psychology, Jung stated in his book
Psychological Types: 'In general, it is the process of forming and
specialising the individual nature; in particular, it is the devel-

---

35. *The Great Mother* (New Haven: Princeton University Press, 1963),
24ff.
36. Calvet, *St Vincent de Paul*, op. cit., 24.

opment of the psychological individual as a differentiated being from the general, collective psychology. Individuation, therefore, is a process of differentiation, having for its goal the development of the individual personality.'[37] On another occasion he wrote: 'Individuation means becoming a single, homogeneous being, and, in so far as "individuality" embraces our innermost, last, and incomparable uniqueness, it also implies becoming one's own self. We could therefore translate individuation as coming to self-realisation.'[38] When Vincent crossed symbolically from his place of captivity in pagan Africa to freedom in Christian Europe, he was a changed man. He had begun to come to terms with his shadowy inferior self, with his repressed femininity, and the unsavory aspects of his persona. Jung says that 'the psychological process of individuation is clearly bound up with the so-called transcendent.'[39] True to form, Jung asserts that relationship with the numinous is the northern star that guides and integrates the individuation process. In Vincent's case it enabled him to move from extrinsic to intrinsic faith.

An Ignatian Perspective

Needless to say, the Jungian interpretation proposed here, is of necessity, tentative in nature. We are on firmer ground when we suspect that Vincent experienced spiritual disillusionment which exposed his shortcomings. In his *Spiritual Exercises*, St Ignatius describes two stages of Christian growth, which are epitomised by the dynamics informing weeks one and two of the *Exercises*, respectively.[40] In the first, the main dynamic at work is that the person is motivated by a self-centred need to re-

---

37. *The Basic Writings of C. G. Jung* (New York: The Modern Library, 1959), 259.
38. *The Basic Writings of C. G. Jung,* op. cit., 143.
39. *The Basic Writings of C. G. Jung,* op. cit., 260.
40. D. Fleming (ed), *A Contemporary Reading of The Spiritual Exercises* (St Louis: Institute of Jesuit Resources, 1980), pars 137-146; Carl Jung says in a 'Letter to Pere Lachat' that he gave a course on the *Spiritual Exercises* of St Ignatius at the Federal Polytechnic Institute Zurich, June 1939- March 1940, in *Psychology and Western Religion* (London: Ark: 1988), 240.

ceive the mercy, love, consolations and the spiritual or material gifts of God. I may say in passing that there is nothing wrong with this kind of desire; it is prompted by the Lord and is a necessary preparation for the second stage of spiritual development. In some respects it corresponds to Allport's description of immature religion. However, a problem arises when individuals get stuck at this stage and, and fail to move on to the second.

In the second stage, the main dynamic, at work in the person, is motivated by a God-centred desire to be united to Jesus as he really is, i.e. poor, humble and dependant on God. S/he no longer focuses on the gifts or consolations of God, but rather on the God of consolation and the gifts. Inwardly, s/he shifts from asking, 'What can God do for me?' to 'What can I do for the God?' There is evidence that this is what happened in Vincent's de Paul's case. During and after his captivity, he shifted from a self-centred to a more God-centred spirituality. I suspect that he came to acknowledge how his worldly desire for money, status and advancement were incompatible with the spirit of Jesus. It would seem that, during this period, he began to be motivated by a desire to imitate Jesus by willingly embracing poverty, humility and dependence on God. He had a growing desire to be united to him by humbly serving the Lord in the poor of his day. We can infer that this dynamic was at work in Vincent's life by the way in which he lived, following his return to Paris, in 1608. As the Lord says, 'By your fruits you shall be known' (Mt 7:16).

3. Purification and transformation 1608-1614

Vincent was 27 when he returned to the capital. As we look at three representative events we will see how much he had changed. The first concerns the way he handled a threat to his good name. He was sharing an apartment with a judge at the time. One day while he was sick in bed, a thief made off with the judge's money. Vincent describes what happened next: 'A member of the community was once accused of having robbed his companion, and that before the house where he was staying.

The charge was not true. Finding himself falsely accused, although he never meant to justify himself, the thought nevertheless did occur to him: "See here; you are going to justify yourself, are you not? You are being falsely accused you know!" "Oh no," he said, as he lifted his mind to God, "it is necessary that I suffer this patiently".'[41] What a change. At 24 years of age Vincent demanded his rights, now he was willing to renounce them even if it meant the loss of his good name.

His attitude to money had also changed. In 1611 he received a gift of 15,000 livres from John Latanne, master of the Paris mint. He immediately gave it to the Charity Hospital 'to tend and nurse the sick poor'. Gone was his earlier preoccupation with cash. In its place is evidence of a growing sensitivity to the poor. However, there is also evidence that Vincent was tempted to resist his growing attraction to a life lived in total commitment to the poor. For example in 1610 he wrote to his mother: 'I put great hope in God's grace, that he will bless my efforts, and soon give me the means of an honourable retirement so that I may spend the rest of my days near you.'[42] Retirement at the age of 29! Vincent still had mixed desires, his purification was not yet complete.

The year 1610 inaugurated another marker event. Vincent knew a priest who was experiencing terrible temptations against faith.[43] Apparently, he prayed that God would allow him to accept this man's burden in return for his peace of mind. Although Bishop Abelly, Vincent's first biographer recounts this incident, José Maria Roman, a modern biographer says that, as his is the only source of the story, it is questionable.[44] What we do know for sure is that the theologian's trial ended while Vincent entered the period of interior struggle. Later he was to say: 'God often wishes to establish, upon the patience of those who under-

41. Purcell, 'St Vincent de Paul: Spiritual Life', *All Hallows Annual* 1959-1961, 55.

42. *All Hallows Annual,* op. cit., 55

43. Cf Luigi Mezzadri CM, *A Short Life of St Vincent de Paul* (Dublin: Columba, 1992), 15.

44. *St Vincent de Paul: A Biography* (London: Melisende, 1999), 100.

take them, the good works that are to endure, and for that reason he allows such people to suffer many trials.'[45] Well, Vincent
battled with doubt and dark moods for about three years.
During this time he learned, with the help of Cardinal de Berulle
and others, to die to the last vestiges of his pride. Finally, as
William Purcell wrote, 'He made up his mind to devote himself
wholly and irrevocably to the service of the poor out of love for
his Divine Master and in order to imitate him more perfectly.'[46]
When his doubts disappeared at this time, Vincent's faith was as
strong as his commitment to the poor was complete. Faith and
commitment found a united focus in dedicated service of Jesus
in the poor and humble.

Conclusion

Over thirteen years or so Vincent had gone through a remarkable interior change. Because of the constraints of space, I have
chosen not to describe many of the significant events that occurred in his life between 1609 and 1614, such as his appoint-
ment as Chaplain to Queen Marguerite of Valois (1610), absen-
tee abbot of Saint-Leonard-de-Chaume (1610), parish priest of
Clichy-la-Garenne (1612), tutor to the de Gondi children (1613).
Suffice it to say that he made the following words of scripture
his own: 'You were taught, with regard to your former way of
life, to put off your old self, which is being corrupted by its de-
ceitful desires; to be made new in the attitude of your mind; and
to put on the new self, created to be like God in true righteousness and holiness' (Eph 4:22-24). Instead of making him bitter,
his many trials had made him better. During his time of passage
he had discovered 'the potency of disorder'. Bit by bit he had become disillusioned with his youthful sense of identity and prior-
ities. He learned to embrace his priestly vocation in a new, more
interior way. As a priest from a humble, peasant background, he
had tried to escape from the implications of material and spiritual
poverty, as from an enemy. But between the ages of 20 and 33 he

---

45. Coste, op. cit., vol. 1, 44
46. *All Hallows Annual*, op. cit., 74.

learned to love this enemy within. When he finally befriended this inner and outer adversary in 1614, he found that it was Jesus he was loving in the guise of the poor of his day. He discovered the truth of the words: 'As often as you did it for one of these the least of my brothers, you did it for me' (Mt 25:44). Vincent was about to commit himself, as a priest, to follow Christ the evangeliser of the poor. Surely the dynamics of his gradual transformation can act as a template for our own journey to sanctity by means of intimate union with the King of the Beggars.

CHAPTER TEN

Spirituality and Near Death Experiences

My late father was a vet in a government laboratory. I can remember him saying: 'There were very few effective medical remedies before the twentieth century.' By and large he was right. Books, such as Roy Porter's *Blood and Guts: A Short History of Medicine*,[1] confirm this impression. But nowadays, thanks to surgery, new drugs and technologies, dramatic progress has been made. One result of all the therapeutic breakthroughs is the ability of the medical profession to resuscitate people whose hearts, lungs and brains have stopped functioning. From a medical point of view, clinical death is a period of unconsciousness caused by insufficient blood supply to the brain because of inadequate circulation. If it is not reversed within 5-10 minutes, irreparable damage is done to the brain and the patient dies.

NDE Research Findings

At least 18% of those whose lives have been saved, have reported having near death experiences (NDEs). They can be defined as the reported memory of all the impressions during a special state of consciousness, including specific elements such as out-of-body experience, pleasant feelings, and seeing a tunnel, a light, deceased relatives, and perhaps a life review. This is a composite account of a near death experience, which includes typical aspects from many others.

A man is dying and as he reaches the point of greatest physical distress, he hears himself pronounced dead by his doctor. He begins to hear an uncomfortable noise, a loud ringing or buzzing, and at the same time feels himself moving very rapidly

---

1. (London: Penguin, 2002).

through a long dark tunnel. After this, he suddenly finds himself outside of his own physical body, as though he is a spectator. He watches the resuscitation attempt from this unusual vantage point and is in a state of emotional upheaval.

After a while, he collects himself and becomes more accustomed to his condition. He notices that he still has a body but one of a very different nature and with very different powers from the physical body he has left behind. Soon other things begin to happen. Others come to meet and to help him. He glimpses the spirits of relatives and friends who have already died, a loving, warm spirit of a kind he has never encountered before – a being of light – appears before him. This being asks him a question, nonverbally, to make him evaluate his life and helps him along by showing him a panoramic, instantaneous playback of the major events of his life. He views the events of his life, not from the perspective he had when he went through the event, but rather from a third-person, empathic point of view. For instance, he takes the perspective of the person that he was unkind to. And if he sees an action where he was loving to someone he can feel the warmth and good feelings that it has produced in the life of that person.

At some point he finds himself approaching some sort of barrier or border, apparently, representing the limit between earthly life and the next life. Yet he finds he must go back to earth; the time for his death has not yet come. At this point he resists, for by now he is taken up with his experiences in the afterlife and does not want to return. He is overwhelmed by intense feelings of joy, peace and love. Despite his attitude, though, he somehow reunites with his physical body and lives.

Later he tries to tell others, but he has trouble doing so. In the first place he can find no human words adequate to describe these unearthly episodes. He also finds that others scoff, so he stops telling other people. Still, the experience affects his life profoundly, especially his views about death and its relationship to life.

May I say that there are many accounts of near death experiences in the literature of the past such as one recorded by Plato near the end of his *Republic*:

> ... the tale of a warrior bold, Er, the son of Armenious, by race a Pamphylian. He once upon a time was slain in battle, and when the corpses were taken up on the tenth day already decayed, was found intact, and having been brought home, at the moment of his funeral, on the twelfth day as he lay upon the pyre, revived, and after coming to life related what, he said, he had seen in the world beyond. He said that when his soul went forth from his body he journeyed with a great company and that they came to a mysterious region where there were two openings side by side in the earth, and above and over against them in the heaven two others, and that judges were sitting between these, and that after every judgement they bade the righteous journey to the right and upward through the heaven with tokens attached to them in front of the judgement passed upon them, and the unjust to take the road to the left and downward, they too wearing behind signs of all that had befallen them, and that when he himself drew near they told him that he must be the messenger to humanity to tell them of that other world, and they charged him to give ear and to observe everything in the place. (Rep. X, 614 b, c, d)

In the sixth century Pope Gregory the Great collected examples of NDEs in his book of tales called *Dialogues*. He made an effort to ensure that the subjects were of good character and not mentally ill. One example was a soldier who nearly died in battle, and had an out-of-body experience. He crossed a bridge over a dark gloomy river, and entered into a beautiful garden with a house of golden bricks.[2] In the eighth century, the Venerable Bede recounted the following experience in his *Ecclesiastical History*:

> He came back to life and suddenly sat up – those weeping around the body were very upset and ran away. 'I was guided by a handsome man in a shining robe,' he said. 'When we

2. C. Zaleski, *Otherworld Journeys* (New York: Oxford University Press, 1987), 26-45, 107.

reached the top of a wall, there was there a wide and pleasant meadow, with light flooding in that seemed brighter than daylight or the midday sun. I was very reluctant to leave, for I was enraptured by the place's pleasantness and beauty and by the company I saw there. From now on I must live in a completely different way.' He later left all his worldly responsibilities and entered the Melrose monastery.[3]

From a scientific point of view these types of experience are very surprising because it was thought that consciousness was completely dependent upon the workings of the brain. If the cortex gave no sign of electrical or chemical activity how could vivid, coherent and meaningful awareness be possible? Over the years an increasing number of researchers have investigated the phenomenon. For example, Denver cardiologist Fred Schoonmaker studied 2300 cases of cardiac arrest and described 1400 of them having NDEs similar to those described by Raymond Moody. The rest of this chapter will mainly examine an article on NDEs in *The Lancet* which was co-authored by four Dutch researchers. It focused on survivors of cardiac arrest in the Netherlands.[4]

The Dutch study came to a number of very significant conclusions. For instance, it discovered that although the average age for NDEs was around 60, the likelihood of their occurrence was higher in younger people, especially children. The research could not explain the occurrence of NDEs in terms of psychological, neurological, biological or medical factors. For unknown reasons, those who had an NDE were more likely to die within 30 days than those who did not. This chapter will not discuss whether the research findings prove that conscious awareness is independent of the brain, or that there is life after death. Suffice it say, that while the evidence indicates that both are likely, there is no certain scientific proof that such is the case. We will focus

---

3. Book 5, chapter 12.
4. Pin van Lommel, Ruud van Wees, Vincent Meyers, Ingrid Elfferich, 'Near-death experience in survivors of cardiac arrest; a prospective study in the Netherlands', *The Lancet*, vol 358, no 9298, (Dec 15th 2001).

instead, on the spiritual effects and therapeutic implications of NDEs.

In the Dutch study, researchers asked resuscitated people 34 questions about such things as self-image, concern for others, social issues, religious beliefs, spirituality and their attitude to death. The interviews were conducted two and eight years after their recovery. All patients, including those who did not have an NDE were more self-assured, socially aware, and religious than they had been before. However, the biggest transformation was evident in those who had an NDE. The Dutch report says that they experienced life-changing insights: 'They were more emotionally vulnerable and empathic, and often there was evidence of increased intuitive feelings. Most of this group did not show any fear of death and strongly believed in an afterlife.' These positive changes were even more apparent after eight years than they had been after two. The Dutch study also discovered that although resuscitation had a positive, overall effect upon those who didn't have an NDE, after eight years their interest in spirituality had sharply declined, whereas it had significantly increased in those who did have an NDE.

Research also indicates that if a NDE is artificially induced by drugs, such as LSD or mescaline, it may lead to an out-of-body experience together with flashes of light and fragmented and random memories. However, it will have neither the coherence or life transforming effects of an authentic NDE. As the Dutch study says: 'transformational processes with life changing life-insight and disappearance of fear of death are rarely reported after induced experiences.'

Hellish NDEs
Many of the books that describe NDEs, especially those which are published by people who are influenced by New Age spirituality, tend to be misleading because they only report positive experiences. However, a number of researchers have maintained that some NDEs are negative in nature. Members of the International Association for Near-Death Studies group at Yale

University Medical Centre have collected at least 50 cases of negative NDEs They have classified them into three groups. Firstly, there are those who during the NDE see the approaching light, not as the reassuring presence of God but as the frightening radiation of the fires of hell. Secondly, there are those who feel trapped by a terrible emptiness, a cosmic nothingness, and thirdly, there are those who have a vision of a hellish place where people are tortured and tormented.[5] In a book entitled, *Before Death Comes*,[6] Dr Rawlings recalls a negative near death experience.

Things suddenly started getting dark, and I found myself spiralling through space into another sort of world; I was travelling very fast. It was some sort of tube that ended in black nothing. I felt like I was being sucked into a big, black void. I was getting hotter and hotter as I was approaching a light coming from a side entrance or a side hole which led to another tunnel which contained long rows of benches with people sitting on them.

They made me sit at the end of one long bench which seemed to stretch for a long distance and angle into another opening or tunnel which was illumined by a brighter light than this one. I couldn't see where the light was coming from or what was in the tunnel, so I asked a fellow next to me, but he didn't seem to know either. He was also waiting his turn. Then I noticed a grimy looking guard standing near the entrance, his arms crossed. As another batch of people left the bench in our room to go into the next room, the figure ordered all of us to move up. Two of the people I saw on the bench I had known in high school. I'm sure of it.

As we moved down the bench, I was close enough to see around into the next passageway, and there in the walls were large doors with iron gratings containing huge fires behind them. Overseers that seemed to have absolute command

---

5. Cf d'Aquili and Newberg, *The Mystical Mind: Probing the Biology of Religious Experience* (Minneapolis: Fortress Press, 1999), 125.
6. (London: Sheldon Press, 1980), 23-24; 127-129.

were rapidly pushing people into these ovens or fires. As one group of people entered, others were moved by drivers in the rear passageways.

I prayed and prayed, 'God help me! God save me!' In some way my name was called out from far above the passageways, vibrating all the way down to where I was sitting. I heard the voice say, 'I have called you back. I have need of you!'

The next thing I knew I was back in my body and looking up into the face of the doctor who was making an awful thrust into my chest that made me feel like my ribs were broken. I really didn't care if he broke all my ribs! I was just glad to be back. I never want to go back to that place! It opened my eyes about how I was living my own life. I've since made a great change. It has made a believer out of me!

Dr Rawlings suggests a number of reasons why so few hellish NDEs are reported. Firstly, those who write books on the subject usually are not present when people are resuscitated. As a result, they don't hear them screaming in distress. Secondly, only volunteers are interviewed, and they tend to tell positive stories. Thirdly, Rawlings believes that hellish experiences are so traumatic that patients push them into their unconscious minds as soon as they recover. As a result they usually have no memories of them. Dr Rawlings found that 18% of his patients reported hellish NDEs.

At the end of 2005 I met a British TV executive who had experienced clinical death for nearly fifteen minutes. During that time he had a life changing religious experience. I was interested to find that he was one of a small number of people who could remember a hellish awareness. In a written account he not only recounted it, he also described its effect upon him:

During that 15 minutes it was made very clear to me that if the Lord had not sent me back I would have spent eternity in hell. My life was full of compromise not only through the work I was doing but in my private life also. I thank God that through his grace he has given me a second chance. I hold onto the words 'not yet David' and know that there were other plans for me. There is a real heaven and a real hell with total separation between the two. I stood in limbo between the two and saw the brightness and glow of heaven and the pressing darkness and total separation from God of hell. Hell is not what you can imagine it is. It's ten million times worse that anyone can ever imagine and more.

NDEs and other Religious Experiences

The noted pollster George Gallup has pointed out that verge-of-death experiences have much in common with other types of religious experience and are probably all on the same spiritual spectrum. While I have never experienced an NDE, I had a strange religious experience, many years ago, which had certain characteristics in common with an NDE.

During a visit to a friend's house I listened to Anton Dvorak's New World Symphony. As I did so, I experienced a three part vision. At first I saw gentle peasants dancing merrily in a field. Suddenly, I became apprehensive when I saw well armed soldiers coming toward them. 'Oh no,' I thought, 'It's always the same. Those with power oppress the innocent and the vulnerable.'

Then the scene changed. I could see that a lot of the peasants had been killed, others were wounded. To my surprise, some of the soldiers were either dead or wounded also. Spontaneously, some words from Ps 55:6 came to mind, 'Oh that I had wings like a dove! I would fly away and be at rest.' Then an inner, but independent voice seemed to say to me, 'If you want me to take you, I will.' I understood that this was God the Father saying to me that he would take me to heaven in the immediate future. While I wasn't frightened by the offer, I looked at the dead and wounded, and replied, 'No, I'd better stay for their sake.' Then I saw the cross of Jesus from behind. Again I heard the inner voice. This time it said, 'Now you have learned the meaning of love. It is compassion. My Son also wanted to fly away and to be at rest, but he

remained for your sake.' I understood that this referred to
Christ's crisis in the Garden of Gethsemane and his willingness to die for us in accordance with the Father's loving will.

Then the final scene appeared. I could see a great orb of
blazing light coming toward the earth. I knew that it was the
presence of the divine Glory. As it grew closer to the earth,
the rocks, soil and plants were bleached as they became radi-
ant with light. My own body was also shining with light. By
now I was rising in the air to meet the approaching orb of
light. At one point I looked back toward the earth. I could see
graves opening and the bodies of peasants rising in glory.
But I was confused when I saw that some of the dead soldiers
were ascending also. I said to the Lord: 'Why should those
who have oppressed the innocent also rise?' The inner voice
replied: 'Because you didn't condemn your oppressors, they
too will be saved!' Then the vision faded as suddenly as it
had begun.

My heart was racing, my breathing was rapid, my spirit
was exultant. I felt that the Lord had revealed a wonderful
truth to me, one that has influenced my attitudes ever since.
God will never be outdone in mercy by creatures. If believers
refuse to judge or condemn those who hurt them, God won't
judge or condemn them either. If we put the scales of justice
aside, and offer the free gift of mercy to those who deserve
condemnation, not only will we be saved, so will they. As
Jesus said, 'Those whose sins you forgive, they are forgiven
… the measure you give to others is the measure you will receive from God' (Jn 20:23; Mt 6:14).

As I have reflected on that experience it has provided on-
going guidance for my life, by prompting me to live in a merciful way. A prayer found scrawled on a piece of paper at
Ravensbruck Concentration camp, encapsulates the attitude I
desire to imitate: 'Lord, don't just remember the men and
women of good will, but also those of ill will. Don't just remember the suffering they have inflicted on us, remember also the
fruits we have borne, thanks to this suffering – our comradeship,

our loyalty, our humility, the courage, generosity and greatness of heart which have grown out of all this – and when they come to judgement, let all the fruits we have borne be their forgiveness.'

NDEs and Spirituality

In an earlier chapter on 'The Paranormal, Disturbed Buildings and Spirituality' I adverted to the fact that in some classifications, NDEs are designated as paranormal experiences. I would question that nomenclature. I see them as religious experiences of mystical intensity. Not only that, they are often associated with New Age spirituality, not because they are intrinsically so, but because New Age devotees are interested in the kind of higher states of consciousness associated with NDEs, especially those of a positive kind.

Like all religious experiences NDEs have many implications. Firstly, because they occur naturally in populations all around the world, regardless of culture or religion, they are a powerful scientific indicator of the central importance of spirituality in our lives. In a culture that tends to focus exclusively on psychosomatic medicine, NDEs are a salutary reminder of the central importance of the spiritual dimension of human experience, what could be referred to as the pneuma-psycho-somatic perspective.

Secondly, I'm convinced that NDEs have important implications for psychology. Firstly, they warn us, if warning is needed, to avoid the reductionist model of interpretation that informs a good deal of western medical, psychiatric and therapeutic practice, in so far as it fails to acknowledge the primacy of the spiritual in human welfare. Fritjof Capra has written in a perceptive way about this reductionist tendency in his book *The Turning Point: Science, Society and the Rising Culture*.[7] It contains an interesting chapter entitled, 'Newtonian Psychology' which, as its title suggests, warns against a strictly rationalistic and mechanistic model of the workings of the human mind. Such a model

---

7. (New York: Bantam Books, 1983), 101-187. 23.

has 'no room for experiences of altered states of consciousness, that challenge all the basic concepts of classical science.'[8] NDEs challenge the adequacy of the Newtonian perspective.

Thirdly, in traditional Catholic spirituality we talk of the purgative, illuminative and unitive stages of the spiritual life. It seems to me that while there may be purgative and unitive aspects to these experiences, the main emphasis is on illumination. It is a vivid, experiential appreciation of the reality of the numinous and things of the Spirit. They may, or may not, have been known beforehand at the level of consciousness.

Fourthly, the spirituality of those who have had NDEs not only tends to have certain characteristics in common, they clearly accord with the teachings of the Bible.

1) People who have had near death experiences have no fear of death. While they enjoy life, and don't want a painful, lingering end, they have no fear of death itself. As Dr Moody attests: 'They don't fear it in the least anymore as being a cessation of consciousness' (cf 1 Cor 15:55).

2) Those who have had a hellish type NDE, usually have a change of heart and try to live better lives (cf Lk 12:5).

3) They don't think that money, material things, roles, status, or success are very important. This point echoes a number of New Testament verses (cf Mt 6:24).

4) Dr Peter Fenwick, a consultant neuropsychiatrist at the Maudsley hospital in London, suspects that NDEs are mystical experiences 'whereby the individual sees through into the very structure of matter itself, and those people who have had these mystical experiences say it is composed of universal love. So they argue for the world being conscious and loving.'[9] People who have had NDEs feel that, self-forgetful, empathic love in relationships is the key value. They desire to treat others in the way they would want to be treated themselves. They are convinced that, as St John of the Cross

8. *The Turning Point*, op. cit., 187.
9. Hugh Montefiore, 'Near-death Experiences', *The Paranormal: A Bishop Investigates* (Leicestershire: Upfront, 2002), 167.

said: 'in the evening of our lives we will be judged on love
and love alone' (cf Mt 25:40.)

5) They live in the present moment. They are not inclined to
worry very much about what happened in the past or is
going to happen in the future (cf. Mt 6:34).

6) Regardless of age, they have a renewed interest in learning as
a means of worthwhile self-development. The wisdom literature of the Old Testament is punctuated with passages about
the pursuit of wisdom (cf Sir 6: 4-37).

7) While they value the religion to which they may belong, they
feel that it is not denominational religion that counts, but
rather, commitment to the core spiritual truths and values
that are embodied in religion, such as being in harmony with
God and one's fellow human beings (cf. Mk 9:39).[10]

Some Implications for Therapists

I'm convinced that NDEs have important implications for counsellors and therapists. Firstly, they warn us, if warning is needed,
to avoid the reductionist model of care that informs a good deal
of western medical, psychiatric and therapeutic practice, in so
far as it fails to acknowledge the central role of the spiritual in
human welfare. As we noted in the opening chapter, a number
of writers have warned the therapists who try to integrate psychology and spirituality that they can end up by psychologising
spirituality rather than spiritualising psychology.

Secondly, those who are engaged in the helping professions
already mentioned, need to foster their own spiritual lives.
Unfortunately some of them appear to be more informed about
therapeutic theory, dynamics and techniques than they are
about the ins-and-outs of spirituality. As the proverb warns:
'You cannot give what you haven't got.'

Thirdly, not only will people in the caring professions meet
people who have had NDEs, they will also meet a sizeable pro-

10. Raymond Moody MD, 'Life After Life' in *Thinking Allowed:
Conversations on the Leading Edge of Knowledge,* ed. Jeffrey Mishlove,
(Tulsa: Council Oak Books, 1992), 361.

portion of people who have had significant religious experiences in their lives. I believe that the transforming awarenesses that are associated with NDEs are present in all numinous experiences in so far as they are intimations of the saving and healing presence of the Beyond that is in the midst of our everyday lives. Therapists need to honour those experiences, and to help their clients to explore their meaning while assisting them to see how to integrate their implications into their everyday lives (cf 2 Cor 3:18). As Viktor Frankl suggested, carers need to engage in logotherapy, i.e. the exploration and appreciation of perceived spiritual meanings in people's lives.

Conclusion

Thanks to medical progress, there is an increasing number of Lazarus type people in our culture, men, women and children who have not only been resuscitated physically, but who have also been enlightened spiritually. In our materialistic culture, they are witness to the supernatural dimension of life. We would do well to listen to them, and to benefit from their testimony.

CHAPTER ELEVEN

A Spiritual Check-up

Many of us have an annual check-up. When the results become available, the doctor usually gives us a pep talk and recommends life-changes such as dieting and taking exercise. While it is good to look after the body in this way, it is even more important to look after the spirit. Surely, we need regular spiritual check-ups. They should look at important aspects of our spiritual lives, with a view to ascertaining what changes might be needed.

There are many ways of constructing a relevant questionnaire. For example, I have discovered that a number of those on the internet are based on a rather arbitrary selection of scripture texts. This one focuses on religious experience as conscious relationship with God, because this sense of ultimate belonging lies at the heart of all theistic and Christian spirituality. Such experiences have four interconnected elements. They are rooted in God prompted desires, which find expression in self-forgetful attention to creation, people and the scriptures. They are fulfilled when the Lord is manifested in one way or another. This sense of revelation can and should have practical effects on the way in which the person lives. This questionnaire is loosely based upon that fourfold structure. It does not intend to focus on such things as the sacraments, sin, and devotion to Mary, important though these are in their own right.

A Questionnaire

You could begin by asking the Holy Spirit to guide your reflection exercise by saying something like this: 'Lord, you enlighten every heart. Enlighten mine to recognise how you have been drawing me to yourself. Help me, not only to appreciate your loving Presence and activity in my life, but also to respond to them appropriately. Amen.' Where applicable indicate whether your answer is:

- Never   = 0
- Sometimes = 1
- Often   = 2
- Always   = 3

1) In our materialistic culture, many people's lives are too extroverted. They are often preoccupied with external things like popularity, pleasure and power. However, there can be no religious experience without introverted awareness of spiritual or transcendental desires for unconditional meaning. The deeper and stronger the desires, the greater the subsequent blessings will be (cf Deut 4:29). Do you have regular quiet times which enable you to become consciously aware of what you really want in terms of your relationship with God? Do you express your desires to the Lord?

2) Do you find it hard to get in touch with the inner voice of your spiritual desires, either because they are being obscured by a moralistic sense of duty – sometimes referred to as 'hardening of the oughteries' – or by the distracting noise of unacknowledged and unresolved negative feelings, such as insecurity, low self-esteem, anger and resentment which may be rooted in the traumas and injustices of the past?

3) Jewish mystic Simone Weil once rightly observed: 'Attention animated by desire is the whole foundation of spiritual practice.' Spiritual seekers need to pay sustained and self-forgetful attention to the twin bibles of creation, people and the scriptures in the belief that they can mediate the mysterious Presence of the One who Dietrich Bonhoeffer said is 'the Beyond in the midst of our everyday lives.' Do you find it hard to pay attention, for any length of time, because you become quickly distracted by the gravitational pull of your own thoughts, feelings and preoccupations?

4) How often are you aware of a benevolent Presence or Power beyond your everyday self? As a person who is conscious of

having slipped repeatedly on the banana skin of weakness, do you ever feel connected to a merciful God who accepts and loves you unconditionally, as you are?

5) Besides being aware of the transcendence of the loving God beyond you, are you also aware of the immanence of the same divine Love within you? (cf 2 Cor 13:5; Eph 3:17).

6) Those who lack religious experience often suffer from a deep-seated sense of alienation and anxiety. In contrast, those who are aware of God usually feel a growing sense of interconnectedness, a joyful sense of relationship with themselves, other people and creation. Is this reassuring feeling of fellowship a characteristic of your consciousness?

7) At any given time a person is either in a state of spiritual consolation or desolation. Describing these states, St Ignatius of Loyola said in his autobiography: 'Desolation is the contrary to consolation. Contrary to peace there is conflict; contrary to joy, sadness; contrary to hope in higher things, hope in base things; contrary to heavenly love, earthly love; contrary to tears, dryness; contrary to elevation of mind, wandering of the mind to contemptible things.' Do you ever experience bouts of desolation?

8) St Ignatius explains that if an inspiration is not from God, it will be associated sooner or later with desolation of spirit. He also points out that God may withdraw consolation as a result of spiritual laziness, neglect of prayer, lack of effort in resisting sin, or because the person is focusing on the consolations of God rather than the God of consolation. More often than not, God allows desolation in cases like these, in order to purify the person and to bring him or her to a point of single minded dedication to the things of God. When you are suffering from desolation of spirit, does it occur to you, that God is trying to purify you in some way or other?

9) Have you a sense of vocation and purpose in life as a result of being aware of the divine providence of the One, who not only has a loving plan for your life (cf Jer 29:11), but is also willing to direct and provide for you, so that you can carry out the plan? (cf Phil 2:13).

10) It could be argued that the exhortation, 'Walk by the Spirit' in Gal 5:16 is the key to an inspired Christian ethic. The kind of spiritual guidance, required to carry out this injunction, can come in different ways, such as an inner prompting, a twinge of conscience, an inspiring scripture text etc. Are you sensitive and docile to such forms of guidance?

11) One of the main ways of walking by the Spirit is to observe the Golden Rule of Mt 7:12 in which Jesus suggested that loving others is a matter of doing to them what we would reasonably want them to do to us. In your relationships with others, is your goodwill informed by an empathic understanding of what they, rather than you, would think is good for them?

12) Genuine religious experience and divine guidance, usually lead to a greater sense of inner freedom. As St Paul observed: 'Where the Spirit of the Lord is, there is freedom' (2 Cor 3:17). Do you find that instead of living your life on the basis of cheerless duty, you are motivated by a personal sense of inner conviction?

13) Those who have a spiritual outlook appreciate the fact that the existence of the world around them and the countless blessings they have received are all the gifts of God. Besides asking the Lord for help, do you express gratitude and appreciation for all the good things you are aware of, by thanking and praising God on a regular basis? (cf 1 Thess 5:17-18).

14) When you become conscious of who God is, and what the Father and Jesus are like, e.g. forgiving, loving, accepting, understanding, and compassionate, do you try to mirror that awareness, by being for others what the Lord is for you, i.e. by being forgiving, loving, accepting, understanding, and compassionate in your dealings with others? (cf Eph 5:1).

15) Do you find that your growing awareness of spiritual truths and values influences the important choices you have to make in your life? Do they incline you to seek justice for others, especially the poor and the oppressed? (cf Jas 2:14-17).

Diagnosis Leads to Remedial action

Religious experiences are to spirituality what food is to cooking, you cannot have one without the other. When you have done your best to answer the fifteen questions about religious experience, you will be more aware of the state of your spiritual health. If you got 0-15 you are in an unhealthy state; if you got 15-30 you are moderately healthy; if you got from 30-45 you are enjoying good spiritual health. It is worth noting that the results are merely intended to be humorously indicative rather than statistically accurate. Just as the doctor would make recommendations on the basis of a physical check-up, so a spiritual director can make recommendations on the basis of a spiritual inventory. I suspect that he or she would encourage you to concentrate on the following four points.

Firstly, in the future try to become more consciously aware of your spiritual desires. Instead of being half-hearted about them, because of competing worldly desires, try to be whole-hearted about them, while expressing them to God in the confident expectation that, sooner or later they will be satisfied (cf Jer 29:12-13).

Secondly, develop a more contemplative attitude, by learning how to pay undistracted attention to the realities around you, and especially to the word of God, e.g. by means of *Lectio Divina*. Do so in the firm belief that they can and will reveal the Reality of the One who created and inspired them (cf Rom 1:20; 2 Tim 3:1).

Thirdly, expect God to reveal the divine presence to you in new and challenging ways. As Is 48:6-8 says: 'From this time forward I make you hear new things, hidden things that you have not known. They are created now, not long ago; before today you have never heard of them, so that you could not say, "I already knew them." You have never heard, you have never known, from of old your ear has not been opened.' Learn to reflect on the religious dimension of your experiences because, as Cardinal Newman once wrote: 'God's presence is not discerned at the time it is upon us, but afterwards when we look back upon what is gone and over' (cf Lk 2:19).

Fourthly, whenever you have a genuine awareness of the presence of God, deepen it through daily personal prayer and reception of the sacraments, while asking yourself the question, how will this experience effect me and the way in which I live? (cf Jas 1:23-24; 2 Cor 3:18; 13:5).

Conclusion

The spiritual check-up proposed here[1] not only aims to help people who answer it to gauge their spiritual state of health, it also aims to help them to see what could be done to improve their spiritual and, therefore, their general well-being. However, the questionnaire is incomplete, experimental and tentative in nature. I'm well aware that it might include other factors such as the communitarian dimension of spirituality and hope for the future.

---

1. First published in *Spirituality* (Nov-Dec 2003), 325-329.

A Significant Correspondence
(see Chapter Four)

A) LETTER ONE: BILL WILSON TO CARL JUNG, JANUARY 23RD 1961

My dear Dr Jung,

This letter of great appreciation has been very long overdue. May I first introduce myself as Bill W., a co-founder of the Society of Alcoholics Anonymous. Though you have surely heard of us, I doubt if you are aware that a certain conversation you once had with one of your patients, a Mr Rowland H., back in the early 1930s, did play a critical role in the founding of our Fellowship.

Though Rowland H. has long since passed away, the recollections of his remarkable experience while under treatment by you has definitely become part of AA history. Our remembrance of Rowland H.'s statements about his experience with you is as follows: Having exhausted other means of recovery from his alcoholism, it was about 1931 that he became your patient. I believe he remained under your care for perhaps a year. His admiration for you was boundless, and he left you with a feeling of much confidence. To his great consternation, he soon relapsed into intoxication. Certain that you were his 'court of last resort,' he again returned to your care. Then followed the conversation between you that was to become the first link in the chain of events that led to the founding of Alcoholics Anonymous.

My recollection of his account of that conversation is this: First of all, you frankly told him of his hopelessness, so far as any further medical or psychiatric treatment might be concerned. This candid and humble statement of yours was beyond doubt the first foundation stone upon which our Society has since been built. Coming from you, one he so trusted and admired, the impact upon him was immense. When he then asked you if there was any other hope, you told him that there might be, provided he could become the subject of a spiritual or religious experience – in short, a genuine conversion. You pointed out how such an experience, if brought about, might re-motivate him when nothing else could. But you did caution, though, that while such experiences had sometimes brought recovery to alcoholics, they were, nevertheless, comparatively rare. You recommended that he place himself in a religious atmosphere and hope for the best. This I believe was the substance of your advice.

Shortly thereafter, Mr H. joined the Oxford Groups, an evangelical movement then at the height of its success in Europe, and one with which you are doubtless familiar. You will remember their large emphasis upon the principles of self-survey, confession, restitution, and the giving of oneself in service to others. They strongly stressed meditation and prayer. In these surroundings, Rowland H. did find a conversion experience that released him for the time being from his compulsion to drink. Returning to New York, he became very active with the 'O.G.' here, then led by an Episcopal clergyman, Dr Samuel Shoemaker. Dr Shoemaker had been one of the founders of that movement, and his was a powerful personality that carried immense sincerity and conviction.

At this time (1932-34) the Oxford Groups had already sobered a number of alcoholics, and Rowland, feeling that he could especially identify with these sufferers, addressed himself to the help of still others. One of these chanced to be an old schoolmate of mine, Edwin T. ('Ebby'). He had been threatened with commitment to an institution, but Mr H. and another ex-alcoholic 'O.G.' member procured his parole and helped to bring about his sobriety. Meanwhile, I had run the course of alcoholism and was threatened with commitment myself. Fortunately I had fallen under the care of a physician – a Dr William D. Silkworth – who was wonderfully capable of understanding alcoholics. But just as you had given up on Rowland, so had he given me up. It was his theory that alcoholism had two components – an obsession that compelled the sufferer to drink against his will and interest, and some sort of metabolism difficulty which he then called an allergy. The alcoholic's compulsion guaranteed that the alcoholic's drinking would go on, and the allergy made sure that the sufferer would finally deteriorate, go insane, or die. Though I had been one of the few he had thought it possible to help, he was finally obliged to tell me of my hopelessness; I, too, would have to be locked up. To me, this was a shattering blow. Just as Rowland had been made ready for his conversion experience by you, so had my wonderful friend, Dr Silkworth, prepared me.

Hearing of my plight, my friend Edwin T. came to see me at my home where I was drinking. By then, it was November 1934. I had long marked my friend Edwin for a hopeless case. Yet there he was in a very evident state of 'release' which could by no means be accounted for by his mere association for a very short time with the Oxford Groups. Yet this obvious state of release, as distinguished from the usual depression, was tremendously convincing. Because he was a kindred sufferer, he could unquestionably communicate with me at great depth. I knew at once I must find an experience like his, or die.

Again I returned to Dr Silkworth's care where I could be once more sobered and so gain a clearer view of my friend's experience of release, and of Rowland H.'s approach to him. Clear once more of alcohol, I found myself terribly depressed. This seemed to be caused by my inability to gain the slightest faith. Edwin T. again visited me and repeated the simple Oxford Groups' formulas. Soon after he left me I became even more depressed. In utter despair I cried out, 'If there be a God, will he show himself?' There immediately came to me an illumination of enormous impact and dimension, something which I have since tried to describe in the book *Alcoholics Anonymous* and in *AA Comes of Age*, basic texts which I am sending you.

My release from the alcohol obsession was immediate. At once I knew I was a free man. Shortly following my experience, my friend Edwin came to the hospital, bringing me a copy of William James' *Varieties of Religious Experience*. This book gave me the realisation that most conversion experiences, whatever their variety, do have a common denominator of ego collapse at depth. The individual faces an impossible dilemma. In my case the dilemma had been created by my compulsive drinking and the deep feeling of hopelessness had been vastly deepened by my doctor. It was deepened still more by my alcoholic friend when he acquainted me with your verdict of hopelessness respecting Rowland H.

In the wake of my spiritual experience there came a vision of a society of alcoholics, each identifying with and transmitting his experience to the next – chain style. If each sufferer were to carry the news of the scientific hopelessness of alcoholism to each new prospect, he might be able to lay every newcomer wide open to a transforming spiritual experience. This concept proved to be the foundation of such success as Alcoholics Anonymous has since achieved. This has made conversion experiences – nearly every variety reported by James – available on an almost wholesale basis. Our sustained recoveries over the last quarter century number about 300,000. In America and through the world there are today 8,000 AA groups.

So to you, to Dr Shoemaker of the Oxford Groups, to William James, and to my own physician, Dr Silkworth, we of AA owe this tremendous benefaction. As you will now clearly see, this astonishing chain of events actually started long ago in your consulting room, and it was directly founded upon your own humility and deep perception. Very many thoughtful AAs are students of your writings. Because of your conviction that man is something more than intellect, emotion, and two dollars worth of chemicals, you have especially endeared yourself to us.

How our society grew, developed its traditions for unity, and structured its functioning will be seen in the texts and pamphlet material that I am sending you. You will also be interested to learn that in addition to the 'spiritual experience,' many AAs report a great variety of psychic phenomena, the cumulative weight of which is very considerable. Other members have – following their recovery in AA – been much helped by your practitioners. A few have been intrigued by the 'I Ching' and your remarkable introduction to that work.

Please be certain that your place in the affection, and in the history of the Fellowship, is like no other.

Gratefully yours,

William G. W.

Co-founder Alcoholics Anonymous

B) Letter Two: Carl Jung to Bill Wilson, January 30th 1961

Dear Mr Wilson,

Your letter has been very welcome indeed.

I had no news from Roland H. anymore and often wondered what has been his fate. Our conversation which he has adequately reported to you had an aspect of which he did not know. The reason that I could not tell him everything was that those days I had to be exceedingly careful of what I said. I had found out that I was misunderstood in every possible way. Thus I was very careful when I talked to Roland H. But what I really thought about was the result of many experiences with men of his kind.

His craving for alcohol was the equivalent, on a low level, of the spiritual thirst of our being for wholeness, expressed in medieval language: the union with God.*

How could one formulate such an insight in a language that is not misunderstood in our days?

The only right and legitimate way to such an experience is that it happens to you in reality and it can only happen to you when you walk on a path which leads you to higher understanding. You might be led to that goal by an act of grace or through a personal and honest contact with friends, or through a higher education of the mind beyond the confines of mere rationalism. I see from your letter that Roland H. has chosen the second way, which was, under the circumstances, obviously the best one.

I am strongly convinced that the evil principle prevailing in

---

* 'As the deer pants for streams of water, so my soul pants for you, O God' (Ps 42:1).

this world leads the unrecognised spiritual need into perdition, if it is not counteracted either by real religious insight or by the protective wall of human community. An ordinary man, not protected by an action from above and isolated in society, cannot resist the power of evil, which is called very aptly the Devil. But the use of such words arouses so many mistakes that one can only keep aloof from them as much as possible.

These are the reasons why I could not give a full and sufficient explanation to Roland H., but I am risking it with you because I conclude from your very decent and honest letter that you have acquired a point of view above the misleading platitudes one usually hears about alcoholism.

You see, 'alcohol' in Latin is *'spiritus'* and you use the same word for the highest religious experience as well as for the most depraving poison. The helpful formula therefore is: *spiritus contra spiritum.*

Thanking you again for your kind letter

I remain

Yours sincerely

C. G. Jung

Index